Thomas K. Johnson, David Parker, Thomas Schirrmacher (ed.)

In the Name of the Father, Son, and Holy Spirit

World of Theology Series

Published by the Theological Commission of the World Evangelical Alliance

Volume 17

Vol 1	Thomas K. Johnson: The First Step in Missions Training: How our Neighbors are Wrestling with God's General Revelation
Vol 2	Thomas K. Johnson: Christian Ethics in Secular Cultures
Vol 3	David Parker: Discerning the Obedience of Faith: A Short History of the World Evangelical Alliance Theological Commission
Vol 4	Thomas Schirrmacher (Ed.): William Carey: Theologian – Linguist – Social Reformer
Vol 5	Thomas Schirrmacher: Advocate of Love – Martin Bucer as Theologian and Pastor
Vol 6	Thomas Schirrmacher: Culture of Shame / Culture of Guilt
Vol 7	Thomas Schirrmacher: The Koran and the Bible
Vol 8	Thomas Schirrmacher (Ed.): The Humanisation of Slavery in the Old Testament
Vol 9	Jim Harries: New Foundations for Appreciating Africa: Beyond Religious and Secular Deceptions
Vol 10	Thomas Schirrmacher: Missio Dei – God's Missional Nature
Vol 11	Thomas Schirrmacher: Biblical Foundations for 21st Century World Mission
Vol 12	William Wagner, Mark Wagner: Can Evangelicals Truly Change the World? How Seven Philosophical and Religious Movements Are Growing
Vol 13	Thomas Schirrmacher: Modern Fathers
Vol 14	Jim Harries: Jarida juu ya Maisha ya MwAfrika katika huduma ya Ukristo
Vol 15	Peter Lawrence: Fellow Travellers – A Comparative Study on the Identity Formation of Jesus Followers from Jewish, Christian and Muslim Backgrounds in The Holy Land
Vol 16	William Wagner: From Classroom Dummy to University President – Serving God in the Land of Sound of Music
Vol 17	Thomas K. Johnson, David Parker, Thomas Schirrmacher (ed.): In the Name of the Father, Son, and Holy Spirit – Teaching the Trinity from the Creeds to Modern Discussion
Vol 18	Mark Wagner and William Wagner (Ed.): Halfway Up the Mountain

Thomas K. Johnson, David Parker,
Thomas Schirrmacher (ed.)

In the Name of the Father, Son, and Holy Spirit

Teaching the Trinity from the Creeds to Modern Discussion

Essays from Evangelical Review of Theology 38 (2014) 2

WIPF & STOCK · Eugene, Oregon

Wipf and Stock Publishers
199 W 8th Ave, Suite 3
Eugene, OR 97401

In the Name of the Father, Son, and Holy Spirit
Teaching the Trinity from the Creeds to Modern Discussion
By Johnson, Thomas K. and Parker, David
Copyright © 2020 Verlag für Kultur und Wissenschaft Culture and Science Publ.
All rights reserved.
Softcover ISBN-13: 978-1-7252-9436-3
Hardcover ISBN-13: 978-1-7252-9435-6
Publication date 12/4/2020
Previously published by Verlag für Kultur und Wissenschaft Culture and Science Publ., 2020

Contents

Editorial
Thomas K. Johnson, Thomas Schirrmacher, David Parker.................6

Why is the Trinity so Difficult and so Important?
Thomas K. Johnson...7

The Consummate Trinity and
Participation in the Life of God
Brian Edgar 19

In the Name of the Father, Son, and Holy Spirit:
Toward a Transcultural Trinitarian Worldview
J. Scott Horrell..33

The Trinity and Servant-Leadership
William P. Atkinson 45

Vestigia Trinitatis in the Writings of
John Amos Comenius and Clive Staples Lewis
Pavel Hošek 58

'Bones to Philosophy, but milke to faith' –
Celebrating the Trinity
Tersur Aben..67

Appendix: The Trinity in the Bible
and Selected Creeds of the Church
Compiled by Thomas K. Johnson 76

Editorial

There was a remarkable phenomenon in the ancient world. A group of people who were self-consciously marginalized, uneducated, poor, and morally questionable became a moral-cultural force that created orphanages, formed the earliest large non-government organizations (NGOs), took care of the weak, started centres of learning, created new forms of art, and later developed a massive body of literature, philosophy, and music. Their own leaders acknowledged their humble beginnings. 'Not many of were wise by human standards; not many were influential; not many were of noble birth' (1 Cor. 1:20). 'Neither the sexually immoral nor idolaters nor adulterers nor male prostitutes nor homosexual offenders nor thieves nor the greedy nor drunkards nor slanderers nor swindlers will inherit the kingdom of God. And that is what some of you were' (1 Cor. 6:10-11). What turned this worthless rabble into a civilization-creating force that survived the fall of empires?

I believe it was the knowledge of God as Trinity. Though we today may trace the roots of the Trinity to the Old Testament, for the early Christians the idea seemed entirely new. And this dogma provided a comprehensive religion and philosophy with culture-shaping power. As religion, the Trinitarian faith addressed the needs of the human heart in a far more satisfactory manner than the many polytheisms and mystery religions, long ridiculed by thoughtful people. As philosophy, the doctrine of the Trinity explained the universe in a manner far more satisfactory than Platonism, Stoicism, or Epicureanism, which ordinary people never understood.

Intellectuals and drunkards could confess their faith/philosophy together and experience how the big questions of history and existence were answered in a creed they could all remember. Swindlers and prostitutes began to discuss the relation among the divine Persons while scholars and rulers asked for baptism and confessed their sins. The humble were exalted while the exalted were humbled.

With the distance of history we can see that the doctrine of the Trinity was the centre of a holistic and balanced newness that changed everything. Across the global missions movement today we see millions searching for a holistic and unified faith/philosophy to respond to numerous social and intellectual needs while also overcoming serious distortions of the faith. This is why we should look again at the doctrine of the Trinity. The Trinity is the ontological core and control for a unified, holistic and renewing Christian faith/philosophy.

So we have collected essays by thoughtful people from several continents and different parts of the Body of Christ. This collection opens and closes with wide-ranging summaries and in between it reflects on the Trinity and our life with God, world view, servant leadership, and the *vestigia trinitatis*, concluding with the text of key Christian confessions on the Trinity.

By discussing this vital topic with us we hope your trust in the Three-in-One is strengthened while Christian minds become more thoughtful and balanced.

Thomas K. Johnson, Guest Editor
Thomas Schirrmacher, General Editor
David Parker, Executive Editor

Why is the Trinity so Difficult and so Important?

Thomas K. Johnson

Keywords: Control beliefs, dogma, distortions of the faith, heresy, creeds, creation, redemption, prayer, discipleship, art

BEING A FULLY trinitarian Christian is very uncommon because it is very difficult—it is also very important. There are several reasons for this situation. The Trinity is more than a few words on our church doctrinal statement, though that is a valuable start. The Trinity is a matter of knowing God in his complexity, totally different from us in our singularity yet radically similar in having personality in his image, then letting this knowledge of God become the pattern of a renewed Christian mind that replaces control beliefs from unbelieving sources that constantly distort our lives.

History and personal experience show that getting to know God as Trinity is always a difficult and dynamic process in tension with our sinful tendencies and the residue of pre-Christian belief systems. It is important because it means getting to know God. It is also important in order to make the faith attractive to our children and neighbours, overcoming the distortions that drive people from the faith. It is worth serious effort.

I Distortions of the Faith

We have in Christian history many distortions that damage our knowledge of God and our witness to the world. As a teenager I listened to people claim that if we 'walk in the Spirit' we will levitate from place to place without using our 'flesh' (meaning our feet), because this was the way Jesus travelled. The proper interest in real spirituality was pursued in a manner that separated the work of the Holy Spirit from the Father and the Son, failing to recognise that the Spirit proceeds from the Father and the Son to mediate our knowledge of the Father and the Son. The total picture of the faith was remarkably similar to some of the early heresies. I observed how this distortion both

---

Thomas K. Johnson (PhD University of Iowa) is Professor of Ethics for Global Scholars, Vice President for Research Martin Bucer European School of Theology, and Senior Advisor to the Theological Commission World Evangelical Alliance. Ordained in the Presbyterian Church in America, he served as a church planter and is the editor and author of many essays and books in English and German, including Natural Law Ethics: An Evangelical Proposal *(VKW 2005),* Human Rights: A Christian Primer *(WEA, 2008). Parts of this text were previously published in Thomas K. Johnson,* What Difference Does the Trinity Make?: A Complete Faith and Worldview *(Bonn: VKW, 2009). Used with permission.*

made people miserable, lacking the joy of salvation, and drove some from the faith.[1]

Since the Enlightenment we have faced various types of liberal theology. Demythologized Christianity rejected the supposed myths in the Bible as unnecessary to faith; Jesus was reinterpreted within the worldview of Existentialism. Marxist Christianity claimed a life of faith would promote a proletarian revolution; the biblical message was appropriated inside the worldview of Karl Marx. National Socialist Christianity thought Christians should support Adolf Hitler as the representative of God's work in the world, reinterpreting the biblical message inside Hitler's worldview. In each example a worldview of a non-biblical origin functioned as a basis for accepting some biblical beliefs which also filtered out acceptance of other biblical teachings.[2]

What unites misguided zeal and liberal theologies is the way whole themes of the faith are missing. In distorted zeal, faith is not guided by a balanced Christian teaching because basic theology is not present. In place of standard Christian teaching, other expectations about authentic spirituality function as control beliefs. In the examples of liberal theology, the biblical faith is misinterpreted because a secular worldview functions as a control belief and filters out parts of the biblical message; much of basic Christian teaching is lacking because it is replaced by parts of a secular worldview.

The problems of liberal theology and misguided zeal are similar, though they look different. When coming to faith people do not instantly give up their previous belief systems. The human mind is never truly empty; certain questions about life and the world cannot be avoided. If people do not have biblical answers, they almost necessarily hold other answers. These old beliefs can continue to function as control beliefs which have authority over what we think we are allowed to believe.

Everyone has control beliefs, fundamental conceptions arising from one's culture or religious background that guide, perhaps unconsciously, what we are allowed to believe. Control beliefs then form a structure of the mind that organizes everything else we believe.

Control beliefs of a non-biblical origin can prevent people from accepting Christ. When people come to faith, old control beliefs may continue in authority; believers may be prevented from accepting parts of the total truth, while old beliefs organize selected themes of the new faith into something alien to Christianity. This is true of both misguided zeal and liberal theology. Major parts of Christian belief are lacking because a previous belief filters out or distorts a theme of the faith.

These recent distortions of the faith

---

1 These observations are inspired by Francis Schaeffer, *The Church before the Watching World*, which is included in *The Complete Works of Francis Schaeffer: a Christian Worldview*, Vol. 4, *A Christian View of the Church* (Crossway Books, 1982).

2 This analysis comes from Helmut Thielicke, *The Evangelical Faith*, Vol. 1, *Prolegomena: The Relation of Theology to Modern Thought Forms*, translated and edited by Geoffrey W. Bromiley (Grand Rapids: Eerdmans, 1974). Believers whose faith and life are distorted in this manner are usually 'of the world', in terms of the evangelical dictum that we should be 'in the world' but not 'of the world'.

bear a crucial similarity to the early heresies faced by the church. The classical heresies of Marcionism, Gnosticism, and Arianism each interpreted and applied the biblical message in light of control beliefs coming from different religious and cultural roots in the ancient world (varieties of Hellenism). Each distortion was a reduction of the content and practice of the Christian faith, making the total Christian faith and life much less holistic.[3]

This being the case, we must ask a series of important questions about control beliefs. What are proper Christian control beliefs to renew the Christian mind, to overcome ancient heresies, liberal theology and distorted spirituality and to organize our faith into a proper whole? What is the right framework for pastoral diagnosis? What control beliefs should we use in our interaction with secular learning? This is why the early church invested such effort into the dogma of the Trinity; knowing the Trinity became the first Christian consciously structured control belief to both overcome distorted zeal and provide a proper filter to replace the secular worldviews.

The articulation of the theory about the Trinity was not only the development of truths in the Bible; it was the attempt to clarify biblical control beliefs which were also tools for pastoral-theological diagnosis to overcome distorted lives by means of pastoral care and teaching. The ancient heresies, modern distorted zeal, and liberal theology destroy the lives of people and institutions. It is important, therefore, to observe that the doctrine of the Trinity was articulated to teach the full counsel of God, address distortions in the faith of believers, to thereby overcome the power of non-biblical control beliefs. The doctrine of the Trinity simultaneously provided a key control belief and a theological tool to diagnose serious distortions of the faith. That is why I love the Apostles' Creed and the Nicene Creed.

It is a mistake to see the Trinity as archaic metaphysical trivia. The Trinity involves knowing God as One and Three. This precise description of God is not speculation; it provides the framework for holistic faith. The New Testament believers knew God in three ways: They knew the Father as the Creator, Sustainer, and Law-Giver; they knew Jesus as the one who taught them, washed their feet, died on the cross and rose again; they knew the Holy Spirit, poured out at Pentecost, who changed them within; and they knew this was one God.

This basic knowledge of God was articulated into theoretical language in the creeds to overcome serious distortions, each of which arose because the biblical message was accepted in light of inappropriate control beliefs. This process must be continued today.

II Developing Trinitarianism Today

Acts 19 describes a remarkable distortion. Paul wondered if believers in Ephesus had heard there was a Holy Spirit. A group of convictions and experiences was lacking because they knew only the Father and the Son. Taking our cue from this problem, it is worth describing the work of each Person.

---

[3] On this see Thomas K. Johnson, *What Difference Does The Trinity Make? A Complete Faith and Worldview* (Bonn: VKW, 2009), 16-21.

In an important way, all of God's acts are the acts of all three Persons. Though we customarily see creation as primarily the work of the Father, both the Son and the Spirit participate in creation. 'All things were made through him', through Christ (Jn. 1:3). 'The Spirit was hovering over the waters' (Gen. 1:2). Though we usually think of redemption as the work of the Son, we often hear good, biblical sermons on the work of each of the three Persons in redemption. Nevertheless, the Bible describes the three Persons as having different roles, and these different roles are summarized in the great creeds.

It is proper to talk about themes contained in first-article faith in 'God the Father, Almighty'. It is also proper to talk about themes contained in faith in second article-faith about Jesus, as well as in the third article about the Holy Spirit. A consciously Trinitarian approach has the advantage of not only being complete; it is also clearly rooted in the most fundamental Christian belief structure about the very nature of God, connecting living faith to proper control beliefs.

In the twenty-first century we can develop a balanced and complete Christian life by seeing the Christian life as knowing the Three-in-One. In this way the doctrine of the Trinity can become the blueprint or outline of the renewed Christian life.[4] We should consider how the Christian life and mind can be structured by the doctrine of the Trinity, so our complete lives can become a conscious response to each Person of God.

When I teach a basic introduction to Christian theology and ethics, I often organize the themes around the relation of each theme to a Person of the Trinity. The following is abbreviated from a course outline. Each paragraph can be expanded as a long study. I learned this method of organizing a course of study from George W. Forell, my doctoral advisor at the University of Iowa, who organized the study of the history of Christian ethics around the way different Christian movements and thinkers emphasized each Person of the Trinity.

1 First-Article faith

A strange question clarifies our thoughts. 'How would life be different if we believed in the second and third articles of the Creed but did not believe in the Father?' That would be strange, perhaps similar to Marcionism and Gnosticism. In reaction we should clarify the first article. When we say we believe in creation, we are saying that God is the only source of all that exists, including matter, energy, time, space, causality, and beauty.

The first article answers the deepest question: What is the ultimate Ground

---

4 So far in Christian history we have had three good attempts to articulate balanced control beliefs that are complementary to each other. The first is the doctrine of the Trinity. The second is the relation between law and gospel. The third is clarifying the relation of creation to the fall, to redemption and ultimate reconciliation. Each can be used to present a summary of the Christian faith in a way that shows that the biblical message has an internal structure which leads to a holistic, balanced, and authentic faith and life. They show that the biblical message is an entire worldview or philosophy.

of Being, the self-existent cause and goal of everything? The question answered by belief in the Creator is so fundamental that if people do not believe in the Father, they ascribe his divine attributes to some part of creation.

When we believe in creation we are saying God gave his creation a specific structure, part of which he built into human nature. The doctrine of creation says much about our world, ourselves and how we should live, about knowledge, and about society. Some biblical themes contribute to a robust first-article faith:

a) The goodness of creation

God made the world good. In Genesis we are told several times that the world God made is good. And 'it was very good' (Gen. 1:31). This theme is emphasized, as if people forget that the earth and the heavens were made by God and are therefore both real and good. Of course this has happened. As noted, the various types of Hellenism doubted the goodness of the physical world. In some types of Hinduism people doubt the reality of the physical world, seeing it as '*Maya*' or illusion. These ways of thinking reappear even among Christians.

b) The creation of humankind

'Let us make man in our image' (Gen. 1:26). Belief that God is our Creator answers the deep question in the human heart: 'Who and what are we?' God created us for a relationship with himself; therefore our human reason, will, and emotions are a created reflection of his uncreated reason, will, and emotions. What a magnificent destiny! How awesome it is to daily interact with other creatures with the same eternal destiny! This is the source of human dignity and meaning, part of first-article faith.

c) The cultural mandate

'Be fruitful and increase in number; fill the earth and subdue it. Rule over the fish of the sea and the birds of the air and over every living creature that moves on the ground' (Gen. 1:28). Everywhere people are busy. They develop careers and families, businesses and schools, cultural institutions and communities. Seldom do we ask, 'Why?' Our activity is not only a human necessity but also a response to the unrecognized demand of God to work in his world. First-article faith recognizes that this demand comes from God, and if we are active in his world, we should be active for his glory.

d) Creation care

'The Lord God took the man and put him in the Garden of Eden to work it and take care of it' (Gen. 2:15). Taking care of God's world and the people who live in God's world is an unavoidable part of our responsibility. As part of first-article faith we recognize that this demand comes from God and should be embraced with joy. As part of the plan coming from our Creator, we expect that a good response from us will contribute to human well-being.

e) General revelation

God continues to speak through his world. 'Since the creation of the world God's invisible qualities—his eternal power and divine nature—have been clearly seen, being understood from what has been made, so that men are without excuse' (Rom. 1:20). God's speech through his creation forms the basis for human accountability to God as it also provides an essential condition for human life and culture. God's general revelation contains much of his moral law, so people often know more than they want to know about the standard they disobey but need (Rom. 1:28-32).

f) Common grace

As part of God's continuing care for his creation, he continues to give humans what is needed for life and civilization. To contrast this gift with the special grace of salvation we often call it 'common grace'. This gift should lead people to repentance and faith. 'Do you show contempt for the riches of his kindness, tolerance, and patience, not realizing that God's kindness leads you toward repentance?' (Rom. 2:4).

It is my speculation that fully knowing God as the Almighty Creator frequently falls from our minds because it emphasizes our radical accountability to God. Even believers sometimes dislike being called to account unconditionally. This makes it important to always talk about the first article.

2 Second-Article faith

Another strange question: how would our lives be different if we did not believe in the second article? How would life be different if we believed only in the Father and the Spirit? Though difficult to imagine, this has happened repeatedly. When people stop believing that Jesus is God in the flesh, God is usually viewed as disconnected from history and uninterested in human needs.

In addition to Arianism mentioned above, one should mention Deism, common during the western Enlightenment of the eighteenth century; God was described as a watchmaker who has finished his work. Deism, like Arianism, was not only a historical movement; it is a recurring tendency among people on the fringe of the gospel.

We should list a few biblical themes that contribute to a robust second-article faith. A life in light of the second article of the Christian creed is a life that fully accepts God's gift in the Cross and simultaneously accepts God's call to take up our cross and follow Jesus.

a) Forgiveness

On the Cross Jesus died for our sins so that we may be forgiven. 'He was delivered over to death for our sins' (Rom. 4:25). Therefore, 'If we confess our sins, he is faithful and just and will forgive us our sins and purify us from all unrighteousness' (1 John 1:9). Forgiveness means release from guilt because Jesus was punished in our place on the cross. The debt was paid by him; since the debt has been paid, it would be unjust if God wanted us to pay again. At its very centre, a true and authentic Christian faith means trust that Jesus paid the price for my sins by his death on the cross. By faith we are freed from guilt before God.

b) Justification by faith

Connected to forgiveness is justification. To make matters more explicit, evangelicals often emphasize that justification is by faith alone, not faith plus something. Paul wrote in Galatians 2:16, 'We . . . have put our faith in Christ Jesus that we may be justified by faith in Christ and not by observing the law.' Justification is a legal term; it refers to the act of a judge in a courtroom declaring a person to be 'not guilty'. It means that the ultimate Judge already gives the eschatological verdict of 'not guilty'.

When God justifies a believer God is not setting aside his own justice. He is declaring that justice has been done and the price of our sins has been paid; Jesus is our substitute in taking the wrath and punishment of God. Faith is the means by which God's gift of justification comes to us.

c) Adoption

'To all who received him, to those who believed in his name, he gave the right to become children of God' (John 1:12). What a tremendous gift we receive by faith in the Son: adoption as children of God! Adoption is similar to our justification; it gives us a legal standing in relation to God, but the gift of adoption goes beyond what God gives us in justification. As the Judge, he could have justified but kept us at a distance from himself. God did not do this.

By so clearly explaining our adoption as God's children, the Bible teaches us that God wants us to have the closest possible intimate personal access to the Father. Our Heavenly Father wants us to call out to him, *Abba*, which means something like 'Papa'.

d) The call to discipleship

'Whoever wants to be my disciple must deny themselves and take up their cross and follow me. For whoever wants to save their life will lose it, but whoever loses their life for me will find it' (Mt. 16:24-25). Faith in the second article of the creed means we have to accept the cost of discipleship and be willing to lose much of what the unbelieving world regards as 'life'. This cost seems small in light of the gifts described in the second article.

e) Jesus as judge

In the Apostles' Creed we confess, 'he shall come as Judge of the living and the dead'. Of course, our Judge is also the one who gave his life for our justification, so we face him without undue fear, knowing his eschatological verdict in advance. It is part of second-article faith to confess that the Son is the Person who both entered into history for salvation and will enter into history for its conclusion.

It is my speculation that even evangelical Christians sometimes neglect the second article of the creed, falling into moralistic deism. We might not like having to admit to ourselves and to God how much we need forgiveness in Jesus.

3 Third-Article faith

Again the strange question: how would our lives be different if we did not know the third Person, the Holy Spirit? What did Paul observe in Acts 19?

How many times the church falls into lifelessness! There is no courage, no love, no authentic care for the needy, no joy in salvation, no desire to glorify God, no pain for those without Christ. The church becomes either a well-ordered machine or the bearer of cultural traditions. Even if our doctrine is orthodox, the light is dim. The criticism of Karl Marx, that religion is the 'opiate of the people', may become true! This damages the witness of the body of Christ in the eyes of a watching world that is looking for authenticity. Do we know the Spirit properly?

'No one can say, "Jesus is Lord", except by the Holy Spirit' (1 Cor. 12:3). Faith is impossible without the Spirit, but our need for the Spirit is continuous. The direct command of the apostle Paul, 'be filled with the Spirit' (Eph. 5:18), may have been written to the same people who had aroused his concern years before in Acts 19. Believers need to be repeatedly filled, regardless of the previous work of the Spirit.

What is the Spirit's work? The Holy Spirit works inside of people, mediating the work of the Father and of the Son as the Spirit proceeds from the Father and the Son.[5] The Spirit changes human consciousness. For example, 'you received the Spirit of sonship. And by him we cry, "*Abba*, Father". The Spirit himself testifies with our spirit that we are God's children' (Rom. 8:15-16).

In this example the Spirit testifies about our relationship with the Father made possible by the Son, yet the Spirit's work is distinct from that of the Father and the Son. This work of God is deeply internal without being subjective or arbitrary, for the Spirit proceeds from the Father and from the Son. Some of the activities of the Spirit are more closely associated with the Father and others more closely related to the Son. A short listing can assist us.

a) The Common work

In Isaiah 45:1-5, we read:

This is what the Lord says to his anointed, to Cyrus, whose right hand I take hold of to subdue nations before him and to strip kings of their armour, to open doors before him so that gates will not be shut. . . . I will give you the treasures of darkness, riches stored in secret places, so that you may know that I am the Lord, the God of Israel, who summons you by name. For the sake of Jacob my servant, of Israel my chosen, I summon you by name and bestow on you a title of honour, though you do not acknowledge me.

Cyrus was a pagan king who did not acknowledge God. Yet he was anointed by the Spirit for a history-changing task, and the word 'anointed' is the same terminology used to describe the anointing of Old Testament priests and kings. Christians call this the 'common' work of the Spirit, mediating the work of the Father in creation, whereas the 'special' work of the Spirit is related to salvation. It is part of how God rules the affairs of peoples and nations.

We should give thanks to God for the common work of his Spirit which has enabled men and women to be leaders in many ways that serve human well-being. Discoveries in medicine, science, and technology which have contributed to the overall human good were not merely human discoveries; the Spirit of God which anointed Cyrus anointed is still at work.

b) The Spirit and art

See, I have chosen Bezalel son of Uri, the son of Hur, of the tribe of Judah, and I have filled him with the Spirit of God, with skill, ability and knowledge in all kinds of crafts—to

---

[5] It was a procedural mistake for the western church to add the *filioque* clause into the Nicene Creed without consulting the eastern church, but it is valuable to know that the Spirit proceeds from both the Father and the Son.

make artistic designs for work in gold, silver and bronze, to cut and set stones, to work in wood, and to engage in all kinds of craftsmanship.... Also I have given skill to all the craftsmen to make everything I have commanded you (Ex. 31:1-6). The Spirit equipped men with gifts of art. The Spirit, who is the unchanging God, can be expected to give similar gifts today. Art, music, and architecture have often flourished among believers, for the glory of God and the comfort and enjoyment of many.

c) The Spirit and life

'The Lord God formed the man from the dust of the ground and breathed into his nostrils the breath of life, and the man became a living being' (Gen. 2:7). The Hebrew words 'breath', 'wind,' and 'spirit' are the same word group. Human life is a distinct gift of the Spirit as the Spirit proceeds out from the Father and breathes life into humans in his image. Sin wrought destruction, bringing a living death; we are born alienated from God, each other, and ourselves.

However, the Holy Spirit has not stopped his life-giving work. He also proceeds from the Son to breathe new life into believers. 'I tell you the truth, no one can enter the kingdom of God unless he is born of water and the Spirit.... "You must be born again"' (John 3:3-7). The Spirit who gives life in the image of God also gives new life in the image of Christ.

d) The fruit of the Spirit

'The fruit of the Spirit is love, joy, peace, patience, kindness, goodness, faithfulness, gentleness, and self-control. Against such things there is no law' (Gal. 5:22-23). Of course we are commanded to do all these things, to practise love, be peaceful, and show kindness. Within ourselves we sense that God created us to image his character in love, joy, peace, patience, and kindness.

The list reminds us that we are commanded by God, created by God, and redeemed by God to be people of the Spirit. However, it is the Spirit of creation, redemption, and the written word who makes the command possible in practice, so we can become fruitful.

Believers often resort to contradictory language to describe life in the Spirit. We use terms like 'the impossible possibility' or 'active passivity' to explain what we experience. Born in sin, it is impossible to live a life marked by this fruit, but the Spirit working in redemption makes possible the purpose for which he breathed life to us in our mother's wombs.

e) The gifts of the Spirit

There are different kinds of gifts, but the same Spirit. There are different kinds of service, but the same Lord. There are different kinds of working, but the same God works all of them in all men. Now to each one the manifestation of the Spirit is given for the common good (1 Cor. 12:4-7).

The Spirit uses spiritual gifts to build the church and society. Unfortunately, controversy about a few gifts easily distracts from the important matter of the faithful reception and use of the wide range of gifts mentioned in the Bible. A few general principles may help.

All believers receive spiritual gifts,

which are particular abilities which we all should use for building up the body of Christ. Each spiritual gift is truly an undeserved gift of God's grace to be received with thanks, but each gift also becomes an area of responsibility.

The use of spiritual gifts is similar to producing the fruit of the Spirit: it requires that we actively strive with all our abilities while we simultaneously look to the Holy Spirit to work through us. We should not make a stark contrast between spiritual gifts and natural abilities, for the Spirit who breathed life into us also breathed new life into us; the same Spirit who created us with natural abilities also gives us spiritual gifts.

f) The Spirit and the Word

'You must understand that no prophecy of Scripture came about by the prophet's own interpretation. For prophecy never had its origin in the will of man, but men spoke from God as they were carried along by the Holy Spirit' (2 Pet. 1:20-21). The image of being 'carried along' was familiar to Peter the fisherman; it was how he saw the sails of his boat filled with the wind. Peter knew how the Scriptures frequently describe the Holy Spirit as the 'wind' or 'breath' of God.

This image implies that men were filled by the wind of the Spirit to write the Bible. They were not turned into mere scribes or word processors, nor were they in some way working on their own, so that their writings were merely their own prophetic interpretation of the will of God. The Holy Spirit filled their sails, meaning their minds and hearts, so that they really were the human writers while the content really was what the Spirit of God desired. If we are interested in the Spirit, we will be interested in the Word.

It is my speculation that even believers may resist fully acknowledging the Holy Spirit because we might not like to admit to ourselves that we need the Spirit's work in us, mediating the work of the Father and the Son to our consciousness. Sin makes us prefer an imagined independence.

III Towards a Trinitarian Life

Responding to each of the Persons of God requires thoughtfulness from us, and this is completely understandable and appropriate. Jesus taught us to love God with our minds, as well as with our heart, soul, and strength. Paul taught us to be renewed by the transforming of our minds.

This thoughtful response will be multifaceted. An important part will be trust: trust in the Father's providential care; trust in the Son's forgiving, justifying work; and trust in the Spirit's comfort and witness to the truth of the Word. Another part will be obedience: serving the Father in the realm of work and culture; imitating the Son in discipleship; and obeying the Spirit's call to use our gifts to build the church by extending the gospel.

Furthermore, a certain part of responding to all three Persons of God is simply a worshipful understanding, impossible without a fully Trinitarian worldview.

We need to ask some questions to develop this thoughtfulness:

1 Is There an Undeveloped Article in Our Creed?

Most readers will affirm the Apostles'

Creed, yet one of the articles of our own creed may be undeveloped. The Christian church is made up of many traditions, each with its strengths and weaknesses. Each Christian family (and even each individual) has its own distinct character or personality which may lead it to neglect a theme of Christian belief.

Some weaknesses result from neglecting a divine Person. A step toward completeness is to assess one's particular faith and part of the Christian tradition; a good way to do this is to ask if an article of the creed is lacking or not well understood. The doctrine of the Trinity is a diagnostic tool.

2 Is There a Disconnected Article in our Creed?

Other distortions result when one of the articles of the creed is disconnected from the other articles. In my youth I disconnected the Spirit's work from the Father and the Son. I saw the Holy Spirit as the source of power and excitement, but my expectations were arbitrary, since I did not know the Spirit proceeds from the Father and the Son to mediate their work to us.

Sometimes we disconnect the work of the Son from the work of the Father and the Spirit, rendering the faith limited in application. In this slightly distorted mode, believers gladly sing, 'Jesus loves me, this I know', but they do not have much more to say. This is a valuable starting point for faith, but the full counsel of God is reduced.

Faith in the Son must be completed by loving the Father and the Spirit. Then the believer recognizes that Jesus calls us to serve and glorify the Father by working in his creation, using all the power and conviction provided by the Spirit. Then we move toward a complete faith.

Some believers are serious about serving God in creation. They are enthusiastic about God's call to glorify him by working for him in society, business, government, family, and education. They talk about the cultural mandate; they love to pursue natural science for the glory of God; and they overflow with gratitude for God's common grace.

Yet they may say little about the joy of justification, there is no enthusiasm for missions, or they let other people talk about the gifts of the Spirit. One wonders if they fully know the Son and the Spirit; deep faith in the Father needs to be completed by a developed response to the Son and the Spirit.

An important step toward maturity begins when we act as if we believe in all three Persons. We should ask if one article of our creed is undeveloped or if we and our churches tend to overemphasize one article of the creed in a way that is largely disconnected from the other two Persons. This process can lead toward completeness and reality in our faith.

3 Practical Steps

Readers should want some specific steps toward a more complete Trinitarian faith. This issue of our journal with its special focus on the topic may be a good step! The next obvious step was already suggested, to use the doctrine of the Trinity as a diagnostic tool to evaluate ourselves and our part of the body of Christ, as Paul did in Acts 19, remembering always that believers are justified before God by faith and must be treated as God's beloved children.

Other steps can include making use of the classical creeds in public worship, trying to give worshippers enough information so they can participate in a well-informed manner. We can use the Apostles' Creed and/or the Nicene Creed in our personal meditation. This will lead us to worship the whole Trinity as we consider the work of each Person.

Finally, we should begin to pray to all three Persons of the Trinity. We may be inclined to pray to the Father or to Jesus, but it is also proper to pray to the Holy Spirit. I have used the doctrine of the Trinity as an outline for theology courses to help students to connect their various convictions and experiences into a coherent whole.

4 The unity and complexity of faith and life

A consciously Trinitarian approach to life and faith will not divide our lives into three. The three Persons are one God, the same in substance, while each Person has distinct functions. So also there should be different dimensions and aspects to our lives, responding to each Person of God, while there is also tremendous unity to our lives, responding to the same God in all of our thoughts, feelings, actions and relationships.

We may have a mistaken blueprint in our minds which guides our thoughts and actions; this blueprint from a religious or cultural movement may act like a control belief which filters out central parts of the biblical belief system. Our fallen minds gravitate in this direction. The Christian mind should accept God's revelation as our filter, so that all other knowledge is judged by and must pass through the filter of God's truth.

The doctrine of the Trinity is central to this process, as good dogma replaces mistaken control beliefs. However, we should notice that being Trinitarian is a dynamic process, never a completed step, as individuals and as the church. It means constantly learning to trust in the Three-in-One.

Let's try being consciously Trinitarian, for the glory of God as well as for our own joy and satisfaction. I think this will also make our faith and life balanced and authentic, therefore more attractive to our children and our neighbours who need the Lord.

The Consummate Trinity and Participation in the Life of God

Brian Edgar

Keywords: Trinity, economic Trinity, immanent Trinity, essential Trinity, consummate Trinity.

THIS PAPER STRESSES the point that if one tries to understand the significance of the eschaton apart from its significance *for God* then one really cannot grasp it at all, for the significance of the eschaton for humanity and the cosmos is tied up with the future eschatological life of God in whom all things come together (Eph. 1:10). Wolfhart Pannenberg commented that, 'it is only 20th century theology that has come to see again the significance of the theme of eschatology for all Christian doctrine'[1] and it remains critically important to continue to stress this in developing an understanding of the nature of God as Trinity. God's kingdom is present in the work of Jesus and shown in his resurrection but its full revelation awaits the end of history, the final consummation, the end of evil, pain and suffering, the fulfilment of human society, the confirmation of divine purposes and the revelation of divine glory.

I Three 'Trinities'

Over many decades now there have been numerous discussions about the *economic* and *immanent* aspects of the Trinity. One central point of debate has been the manner in which the life of God relates to salvation history and whether that connection dissolves the notion of a God who exists independently of creation if the divine life is tied too tightly to the events of salvation history, or whether that is, in fact, the distinctive Christian understanding of the nature of God. With the concept of the *consummate* Trinity I follow Paul in his description of God's plan for the fullness of time to gather all things in Christ found in the first chapter of Ephesians.

In this we see implications for the entire cosmos, but we can also ask

---

[1] Wolfhart Pannenberg, *Systematic Theology*, Vol. 3 (Grand Rapids: Eerdmans, 1998), 532.

Brian Edgar (MTh, Australian College of Theology; PhD, Deakin University) is Professor of Theological Studies at Asbury Theological Seminary (USA) although he primarily resides in Melbourne, Australia. He conducts intensives when in the US and on-line education when in Melbourne. He is the author of God is Friendship: A Theology of Spirituality, Community and Society *(Seeedbed, 2013),* The Message of the Trinity *(IVP, 2004), editor of a number of other books and author of numerous journal articles. An early, somewhat different, version of the table appeared in 'What Hope is there for Mission?' in* Australian Journal of Mission Studies, *Vol. 4, No.2 (December 2010) 55-61.*

about the implications *for God*. This is the ultimate coming of God and his kingdom. The kingdom present is real, but it is still only an anticipation of God's ultimate reign. The notion of the consummate Trinity fills out the significance for God of the *anakephalaiosathai*—the gathering together described in Ephesians 1:10 by which the whole cosmos comes 'under' the head of Christ.

Despite the language of 'economic', 'essential' and 'consummate' Trinity, there is but one Trinity. The term economic Trinity is a reference to the Trinity of salvation and sacrifice, the One who is Creator, Redeemer, and Sustainer, known by the revelation of God's work *within* the created order. The immanent (or 'essential') Trinity is the Trinity of relationship, the origin, the source of life, Father, Son and Spirit, God known by reference to the intrinsic nature of the inner relationships who existed *'before'* creation. These dimensions of the divine nature are well known and their relationship frequently discussed.

The term consummate Trinity is a reference to the Trinity of completion with emphasis on doxology and the integration, the 'bringing together' of all life in God that takes place *'after'* this world. This is Trinity on the far side of the sending of the Father, and beyond the incarnation, cross and resurrection of the Son, and beyond the life-giving mission of the Spirit. This is the Trinity of Glory that includes God's own ultimate and final relationship to the world that is taken *into* the divine life. This is the Trinity with all things gathered together in God.

With a recognition of all the limitations of time-bound language one can say that the immanent life of God gives rise to, or overflows into, the economic activity of salvation and the economic becomes the immanent which takes on, or perhaps takes in, created life and becomes the consummate, fulfilled, completed, perfected Trinity. The implication for humanity is that it, along with the whole of creation, is taken up into the divine life. Life is lived in God for through Christ humanity is able to 'participate in the divine nature' (2 Peter 1:4). Specific reference to the consummate Trinity means emphasising the fact that God's very nature is correlated to the created world through incarnation and atonement, taking human life into the life of God. The divine life is not constituted by the world (as process theology affirms), but neither unaffected by the world (as though the incarnation and the cross were events external to the divine nature).

What are the practical implications of this? The doctrine of the Trinity teaches us about three dimensions of life. The first is personal in that the doctrine of the Trinity, as well as being a doctrine about God, is also an account of the consummate nature of the Christian life. Human life finds its destiny within the life of God. The eschatological implications for the present relate to the manner in which we anticipate, in the way we live now, this future destiny.

The second dimension is social because the Trinity explains to us the nature of human relationships in the light of divine relationships. It guides us in thinking not only about the proper life of the church, but also about the appropriate form for society. The doctrine of the Trinity also has implications for the *cosmic* dimension in that it reveals the

The Trinity understood as -	The Trinity	Dimensions of life	The focus of salvation	Central concepts concerning Trinitarian relations	Imagery	Mission understood as -	Holiness as
'Economic' – describing the specific work of Father, Son and Spirit	Reveals God's *plan* of salvation	Personal	Eternal Life	*Homoousios* (Jesus is "of the same substance" as the Father)	Found in individual objects or persons. A *mark* pattern or stamp. Clover, river, light, force field or person	*Individual* Evangelism Word Conversion	Repentance *Faith* Justification
'Essential' - Describing the inner-life community relationships of the Trinity	Is a *paradigm* for community life	Social	Kingdom of God	*Perichoresis* (Father, Son and Spirit live in community in one another)	Found in relationships. *Model* Community.	*Community* Peace/justice Model; action, transformation	Social *Love* Sanctification
'Consummate' – describing the 'future of God' whereby all things are in Christ	Involves *participation* in the life of God	Cosmic	New Creation	*Anakephalaiōsasthai* (all things gathered together under one head) *Theias koinōnoi phuseōs* (We become 'participants of the divine nature')	Found in Christ. *Membership*.	*Cosmic* Doxology Worship; ecological care,	Participation Divinisation *Hope* Perfection

intrinsic value and doxological purpose of creation.

The rest of this article will develop this understanding of the consummate Trinity by reference to the table which outlines the emphases of the three forms of trinitarian thought. This will involve summarising the frequently discussed implications associated with economic and essential trinitarianism before considering the implications of the consummate Trinity. There are problems associated with this kind of tabular simplification and my only defence is that if one included everything in every part then it wouldn't be possible to have a simple model. The text will provide details that are difficult to express in a table.

II The Economic Trinity

In considering the table it is best to start with the row considering the Trinity understood as 'economic'—describing the specific work of Father, Son and Spirit. Theology has spoken extensively of the economic Trinity which is an understanding of the way God works in the world as Creator, Redeemer and Sustainer in order to bring salvation: God the Father Almighty, Maker of heaven and earth; Jesus Christ the Redeemer of the world; the Holy Spirit, revealer, inspirer, strength and comfort. An initial focus on an economic understanding of the Trinity is perhaps inevitable, given the soteriological focus of the New Testament.

This is by no means separated from an immanent trinitarianism for it is precisely the Father who sent the Son and the Spirit to bring salvation to the world but, from a human point of view, it is the message of salvation which comes first and which requires attention regarding the one from whom, and through whom, this message and this possibility come. The economic Trinity is a statement about the revelation of God's plan of salvation (as in the second column) and this is usually (though certainly not universally) interpreted in primarily personal categories (as per the third column) with the focus being upon the possibility of eternal life for those who believe (column four).

In historical terms there were numerous debates about the nature and the mode of salvation (such as the way good works were involved and whether salvation included the body) but the most critical issues were distinctly trinitarian in nature (for example, whether the God of the Old Testament was the God of the New, and whether the Spirit was divine) with the absolutely central issue concerning the person of Jesus. That is, if Christ is to bring salvation it seemed to many that he must be both God *and* man. The issues involved in this were at the heart of the early church debates about Christ and it was problematic for many.

The debate swung around the word *homoousios* (see column 5): can we say Jesus is 'of the same substance' as the Father—and thus truly God? The orthodox answer was, 'Yes, not only can we, but we must'. As T. F. Torrance says, the *homoousion* 'is of staggering significance. It crystalizes the conviction that while the incarnation falls within the structures of our spatiotemporal humanity in this world, it also falls within the life and being of God.' Consequently, the *homoousion* 'is the ontological and epistemological lynchpin of Christian theology. With it, everything hangs together; without it, everything ultimately falls apart.'²

The most ancient way of illustrating the relationship of the Trinity to the person is that the Trinity is understood as a *mark* (or pattern; see column 6) that is imprinted on the world. This is the *vestigia Trinitatis*—the notion that the fingerprints of the creator, the vestiges of the Trinity, can be seen, by the discerning, in the world around us. This gives a trinitarian character to the whole of creation which may be seen in a three-leafed clover or in the spring of water which gives rise to the river and ends up in the lake: three-in-one and on-in-three.

The idea remains today in popular thought though it is frequently critiqued, but newer versions also exist, particularly within the science-faith dialogue. There is Pannenberg's interpretation of the Spirit as force field,³ Moltmann's ecological concept of space,⁴ Denis Edwards' use of evolutionary emergence,⁵ Happel's use of space-time relations⁶ and Ted Peters' description of the end of the universe.⁷

The early Fathers of the church, however, soon recognised that vestiges of the Trinity that are found in the natural world are less adequate for understanding God because they are not personal enough. This led to the view that the imprint of God is best seen in the highest part of creation—human nature—through the presence of the *imago dei* (Gen 1:26). From Augustine onwards the most important vestiges of the Trinity are seen in the human person (including lover, loved and love; being, knowing and willing; memory, understanding and will).⁸

What practical implications are to be drawn out of this description of the Trinity in economic terms? In terms of *mission* (see column 7) the salvation that is at the heart of an economic interpretation of the Trinity is all about the possibility of eternal life for everyone. In the evangelical tradition salvation is simply, 'The saving of man from the power of sin'.⁹ There are numerous areas where there are debates and differences of opinion concerning aspects of this salvation but the main points are clear.

There is an emphasis, first of all, on the grace of God and the work of Christ in achieving salvation. This is at the heart of economic trinitarian theology. This leads to a reflection on the comprehensiveness of the salvation that overcomes sin, death and judgment

---

2 Thomas F. Torrance, *The Ground and Grammar of Theology* (Edinburgh: T. & T. Clark, 1980), 160–161.
3 Pannenberg, *Systematic Theology*, 1998, 3:82.
4 Jürgen Moltmann, *God in Creation: A New Theology of Creation and the Spirit of God* (Minneapolis: Fortress Press, 1993), 100.
5 Denis Edwards, *The God of Evolution: A Trinitarian Theology* (New York: Paulist Press, 1999).
6 S. Happel, 'Metaphors and Time Asymmetry: Cosmologies in Physics and Christian Meanings', in *Quantum Cosmology and the Laws of Nature* (Vatican City State: Vatican Observatory, 1993), 103–134.
7 Ted Peters, 'The Trinity In and Beyond Time', in *Quantum Cosmology and the Laws of Nature* (Vatican City State: Vatican Observatory, 1993), 263–292.
8 Augustine, *The Trinity* (Washington: Catholic University of America Press, 1963).
9 Walter A. Elwell, *Evangelical Dictionary of Theology* (Grand Rapids, Mich.: Baker, 1984), 967.

and a stress on the value attributed to the human person and God's concern for every individual and the related need for themes such as repentance, individual responsibility, conversion and the place of faith. It culminates in the comprehensive transformation of the individual and a personal resurrection at the final consummation of all things.

Holiness (see column 8), in terms of economic trinitarianism, focuses on the development of the individual: a person's set-apartness for God, their relationship with God and the moral content of their character. Again, there are debates about the distinctives, various emphases and the processes involved, but the fundamental characteristics of inward holiness and external behaviour—sanctification in every aspect of being—are clear.

This outline of the mission of the church and the life of the believer within the context of an economic trinitarianism makes the strengths of this approach very clear. However, it has now long been recognised that this form of presentation of the work of God in salvation is connected with an understanding of mission and holiness that is limited in scope. Those themes that are connected with an immanent, or essential, trinitarianism are required to enhance the understanding of salvation.

III The Essential Trinity

The central truth of the essential Trinity is that God has not merely *appeared* in a trinitarian fashion in order to save the world but is *actually* trinitarian in nature. It directs attention to the essential, inner life of God as Father, Son and Holy Spirit and the focus shifts from the plan of salvation to these inner relationships as a *paradigm* for the life of the church. The relationships between Father, Son and Spirit (as in John 17:20-21) provide a pattern for community relationships and this, in turn, draws attention to the social dimensions of life that God is concerned about—along with individuals.

Historically speaking, if *homoousios* was critical for economic trinitarianism then the equally critical word for immanent trinitarianism has been *perichoresis* which refers to 'mutual indwelling' or 'inter-penetration' of the Father, Son and Holy Spirit. At least since John of Damascus it has meant that there is no separate essence of God apart from God's life as Father, Son and Holy Spirit who live in a communion of persons.

Whereas the imagery for economic trinitarianism was found in various *marks* imprinted on, firstly, the natural world and then, secondly, the individual person, the imagery for essential trinitarianism is found in the social relationships of Father, Son and Spirit that become a *model* or paradigm for the way in which the church is to live. Consequently, corporate imagery, such as the notion of the Kingdom of God, comes to the fore in this thinking.

And what then are the practical implications of an essentialist perspective on trinitarian theology? Inevitably they relate to the social, rather than individual, life of believers and the church. Mission becomes a much more socially orientated activity in which social needs, such as the need for peace and justice predominate. The church is a foretaste of God's community—an eschatological community working for the good of society, ending poverty and doing justice.

This emphasis and the contrast this makes with the notion of salvation typically associated with economic trintarianism has produced the debate about whether mission is really evangelism or social action. The answer is that both of them are grounded in different aspects of the trinitarian nature of God and one ought not to choose just one dimension of mission any more than one should choose between economic and essential dimensions of the Trinity. The absolute unity of the two is well expressed in the Micah Declaration on Integral Mission which says,

> It is not simply that evangelism and social involvement are to be done alongside each other. Rather, in integral mission our proclamation has social consequences as we call people to love and repentance in all areas of life. And our social involvement has evangelistic consequences as we bear witness to the transforming grace of Jesus Christ.[10]

Similarly, there are corporate implications for the understanding of holiness, frequently expressed in terms of *social holiness*. Two different meanings are actually attributed to the term. They need to be distinguished but both are important aspects of the corporate nature of holiness and both derive from the communal nature of the essential Trinity.

The term, 'social holiness', is frequently used with respect to John Wesley's well-known observation in the introduction to the first volume of the Methodist Hymn book that 'the gospel of Christ knows of no religion but social, no holiness but social holiness' and this is commonly connected with the historical reality that Methodism spoke out about the social injustices of the age. Thus 'social holiness' is interpreted as 'social justice' and usually intended as a supplement and a corrective to modern, often evangelical notions of 'personal holiness' that pay little attention to broader community concerns.

The appropriateness of this has increasingly been recognised but it is likely that the phrase as used by Wesley in the hymnbook (and this is the only place he used it) should be interpreted as referring to a different corporate dimension of holiness: the necessarily *social context* in which personal holiness is necessarily formed.[11] That is, no holiness (whether focused on the inner life, the development of character, one's relationships with others or on concerns for social structures) can develop without the influence and the aid of others. One's holiness is not purely and simply one's own; it is dependent, to a significant degree, upon the holiness (or lack of it) of others.

Holiness is social in terms of its growth and development as well as its expression in the world. Altogether, mission and holiness take on different dimensions when considered in the light of the essential relationships of the Trinity as well as in the light of the work of salvation. Together they provide an holistic approach to the life of

---

10 The Micah Network (Sept. 2001) http://www.micahnetwork.org

11 Andrew C. Thompson, 'From Societies to Society: The Shift from Holiness to Justice in the Wesleyan Tradition', *Methodist Review* 3 (2011): 141–172.

the believer, one that is to reflect, in its own appropriate way, the life and the work of the trinitarian God.

These two dimensions of thought concerning the Trinity must be held together. It is well recognised that Karl Barth was largely responsible for reviving the structural significance of the doctrine of the Trinity. His revelational trinitarianism demonstrated the importance of using the doctrine of the Trinity for theological structure. Jürgen Moltmann was also significant in the revival of trinitarian theology and despite the presence of some who have disagreed with this approach they have been followed by a wide range of people looking at the significance of the Trinity for various aspects of life including the church (Miroslav Volf),[12] society (Gordon Kaufman),[13] the cosmos (Sallie McFague),[14] the person in society (Leonardo Boff),[15] community (Stanley Grenz),[16] mission (Lesslie Newbigin),[17] and gender (Kevin Giles).[18]

There has also been significant debate about the relationship between the economic and the essential 'Trinities'. Karl Rahner's well-known rule is that 'the economic Trinity is the immanent Trinity and the immanent Trinity is the economic Trinity'. Ontologically speaking, there is only one Trinity and the language of the economic Trinity and the immanent eternity is really a shorthand way of talking about different aspects or dimensions of God as Trinity. To speak of the economic Trinity is to speak of God's relationship to the world. To speak of the immanent Trinity is to speak of God's inner self.

Yet Rahner's rule has created concerns for some, such as John Thompson[19] who argues that this rule inevitably means that God's existence as Trinity is tied to God's actions in the world and therefore that there is no genuine life of God apart from the world. That is, there is a loss of the immanent. Whether Rahner, LaCugna or Moltmann or others can be read in this way and whether this is what they intend is a matter for debate regarding each one. However, the overall point is that the relationship of economic and immanent perspectives on the Trinity has profound implications for church and society that must continue to be worked through.

I would suggest, however, that trinitarian theological thinking has had less impact upon the local church than upon the theological academy because of the on-going impact of individualism upon the thinking of ordinary Christians in terms of understanding

---

12 Miroslav Volf, *After Our Likeness: The Church as the Image of the Trinity* (Grand Rapids, Mich.: William B. Eerdmans, 1998).

13 Gordon D. Kaufman, *In Face of Mystery: A Constructive Theology* (Cambridge, Mass.: Harvard University Press, 1995).

14 Sallie McFague, *The Body of God: An Ecological Theology* (Minneapolis: Fortress Press, 1993).

15 Leonardo Boff, *Trinity and Society* (Eugene, Ore.: Wipf & Stock Publishers, 2005).

16 Stanley J. Grenz, *Rediscovering the Triune God: The Trinity in Contemporary Theology* (Minneapolis: Fortress Press, 2004).

17 Lesslie Newbigin, *The Open Secret: An Introduction to the Theology of Mission* (Grand Rapids, Mich.: Eerdmans, 1995).

18 Kevin Giles, *The Trinity & Subordinationism: The Doctrine of God and the Contemporary Gender Debate* (Downers Grove, IL: InterVarsity Press, 2002).

19 John Thompson, *Modern Trinitarian Perspectives* (New York: Oxford University Press, 1994), 28.

God. Even when trinitarian in theory (according to formal beliefs) few are instinctively trinitarian in thought or practice. Most Christian thought is, in pragmatic terms, 'personal' or 'individual' ('What does this mean *for me*?'). Much preaching is individualist in structure and aimed at individuals in content.

It is perhaps a rare thing for congregations to begin even to address the full implications of the doctrine of the Trinity. James Torrance, for instance, has pointed out that, even when liturgical language is Trinitarian, often the understanding of worship itself is monotheist with a structure that would be suitable for a Jewish or Muslim person. That is because the structure of worship is unitarian in form in that pastor/priest and people are on one side, offering worship to God who is on the other side, hearing the prayer and receiving the worship.

However, genuinely trinitarian worship is the gift of participating through the Spirit in the incarnate Son's communion with the Father. Trinitarian worship means having God coming onto our side and lifting us up so that worship is fellowship (or participating or sharing) in the life of God. The Trinity, in distinction to other forms of worship, thus provides 'a participatory understanding of worship and prayer'[20] that is predicated on the grace of God rather than on the work, effort or enthusiasm of the believer. In this, and in so many other areas of the church's life, the full implications of essential trinitarianism need to be explored.

IV The Consummate Trinity

Torrance's participatory understanding of worship illustrates the way in which it is possible to incorporate an eschatological dimension into trinitarian thought, but many other discussions do not do this. A more specific focus upon the eschaton and the consummation of all things and the implications of this for the life of God is necessary.

This means taking very seriously Pannenberg's observation that theology has to see again the significance of the theme of eschatology for *all* Christian doctrine.[21] A consideration of God 'at end of time'—the consummate Trinity—is a reflection on God who has embraced within God's own life the whole of creation, and is one that unites economic and immanent dimensions of trinitarian thinking in the eschatological life of God.

This approach to the doctrine of the Trinity goes beyond both the idea of the Trinity as a *mark* on creation and as a *model* for life and sees the doctrine of the Trinity from the inside—by which people, and indeed ultimately the whole of creation—are *members* or partners who participate in communion not only with, but within, the life of God. The life of the Trinity is an interpersonal fellowship in which believers participate by grace. This experiential, participatory understanding of consummation life is a reminder that the future is not so much a *place* as an *existence in God*.

Just as the focus of economic trinitarianism revolved, theologically, around the *homoousios* and the focus

---

[20] James Torrance, *Worship, Community & the Triune God of Grace* (Downers Grove, Ill.: InterVarsity Press, 1996), 9.

[21] Pannenberg, *Systematic Theology*, 1998, 3:532.

of immanent trintarianism can be said to revolve around the concept of *perichoresis*, the concept which is at the heart here is the notion of *anakephalaiosathai*—the 'gathering together' described in Ephesians 1:10 by which the whole cosmos comes 'under' the head of Christ. The very long, complex, single sentence of the first chapter of Ephesians 1: 3-10 reaches its climax in verse 10 in which the Father reveals 'the mystery of his will' (v. 9) to be 'a plan for the fullness of time', namely, 'to bring all things in heaven and earth together under one head, even Christ'.

This 'gathering together' is the *anakephalaiōsis*—a word which occurs only twice in the New Testament. It has the sense of 'bringing things together' so that it can be translated: 'that he might gather together in one all things in Christ' or 'to unite all things in him'.[22] It is also possible to take the basic meaning as relating to the 'head' (*kephalē*) under which all things are brought and so it can be expressed as bringing all things 'together under one head'. Recent scholarship prefers to think of it as referring to the 'main point', 'summary' or perhaps 'heading' in the sense that everything is 'summed up in Christ'. Eugene H. Peterson puts it as 'a long-range plan in which everything would be brought together and summed up in him'.

This summation is not just a summary in the sense of a condensation such as one might have in a brief chapter summary of a text book. Ernest Best suggests it sums up more as an architect's plans sum up a building—it summarises it *and* determines its shape.[23] The only other NT occurrence of this expression is in Romans where Paul says that all the commandments of the law 'are summed up in this one rule: "Love your neighbour as yourself".'

If we draw a parallel here we might say that just as Romans 13:9 shows that all that is true, meaningful and significant for human discipleship in the myriad principles and commandments of the law is expressed in one single command, so Ephesians 1:10 shows how all of God's truth, goodness and purpose that are found throughout the various elements and dimensions of the universe are summed up in the person of Jesus Christ.

However it is put, it is clear that it refers to nothing short of cosmic re-unification in Christ. All things point to Christ—he is the focal point of the whole of creation—and Paul urges people to bring their lives into conformity with God's divine plan so that Christ is central in everything that they do.

In this we see implications for the entire cosmos, but we can also, once again, ask about the implications for God. If we try to understand the significance of the eschaton apart from its significance for God then we really cannot grasp it for the significance of the eschaton for the cosmos is tied up with the future eschatological life of God. At the end, the love of God is victorious, it is the end of tears and suffering (Rev. 21:4) and God enters into fellowship with the whole creation. It is precisely in God that all things come together

---

22 As in, respectively, the AV (King James) and RSV editions.

23 E. Best, *Ephesians* (Edinburgh: T. & T. Clark, 1998), 142.

(Eph. 1:10) and so there is then, as a result 'one God and Father of all, who is above all and through all and in all' (Eph. 4:6).

This dimension stresses the utter *comprehensiveness* of what God is doing in that not only human life but the whole of creation is gathered up. It also stresses the *continuity* of this life in God with the present world. The creation of a new heaven and a new earth does not mean the total abandonment of the old heaven and the old earth. This willingness to gather together all things is a continuation and consummation of the *sacrifice* expressed in the self-giving of the son for the sake of the world. There is a sense in which God sacrifices the divine life to embrace the world in eternal union. The divine nature is thus related to the world 'internally' (through personal relationship) and not merely externally (as a completely separately existing entity) in a consummation of the movement begun with the incarnation.

The notion of the consummate Trinity makes it clear that holiness is *ultimately about participation in the life of God*. The development of virtue and character is important, as are works of social justice, but both are to be directed towards a comprehensive fulfilment of the love relationship with God—whose essential nature is love—begun in relationship with Christ ('whoever lives in love lives in God', 1 John 4:16). The precise nature of a participatory interpretation of the consummation and the significance of, for example, the following passages has been much debated in recent times.

My prayer is not for them alone. I pray also for those who will believe in me through their message, that all of them may be one, Father, just as you are in me and I am in you. May they also be in us so that the world may believe that you have sent me (John 17:20-21).[24]

Through these he has given us his very great and precious promises, so that through them you may participate in the divine nature and escape the corruption in the world caused by evil desires (2 Peter 1:4).

While it is well accepted that the life of the Trinity is to be worked out relationally, the implications beyond that remain controversial. For some *perichoresis* describes the inner, immanent life of God only, but for others it does much more. Just as the economic Trinity, in the work of salvation through suffering and death has implications for God as well as humanity, so too, it is argued that *perichoresis* and the imminent Trinity have implications for human life as well. Those who have developed it include Karl Rahner,[25] Catherine Lacugna[26] and Jürgen Moltmann.[27]

Though not without criticism, Rahner, for example, stressed the notion that God's involvement in the world is so intimate that the character of divinity itself is shaped by it. God's action through Christ in the incarnation redefines divinity to include humanity, and God's work in the Holy Spirit which

---

24 New International Version throughout, except where specified.

25 Karl Rahner, *The Trinity* (New York: Crossroad Pub., 1997).

26 Catherine Mowry LaCugna, *God for Us: The Trinity and Christian Life* (New York: HarperSanFrancisco, 1993).

27 Jürgen Moltmann, *The Trinity and the Kingdom: The Doctrine of God* (Minneapolis, MN: Fortress Press, 1993).

binds believers to Christ means that they are at one with Christ and so, at one with God, and thus, participants in the life of the Trinity.

Moltmann is well known for his desire to ensure that the significance, particularly the pain, of the cross, which is so central to his theology, not only belongs to, but actually constitutes the nature of the Triune God. This means that the history of God in the world constitutes the being of God. This noble quest—to find the cross of Jesus in the heart of God, so that the cross is not external to God—is critiqued by Pannenberg who argues that making the immanent nature of God subject to the life of God in the world actually makes the Trinity devoid of meaning, for the Trinity has significance only if the God revealed in salvation history is the same as God from eternity.[28]

The fact is that despite this conflict of opinion both Moltmann and Pannenberg are seeking to defend the inner nature of God: Moltmann is stressing the importance of self-sacrifice as constitutive of eternal, divine being; Pannenberg is stressing the importance of the eternal nature of the self-sacrificing God.

LaCugna wants to stress the notion that the doctrine of the Trinity—whether understood from economic or immanent perspectives—is not primarily a doctrine about God in isolation but a doctrine about God *in relation to humanity*. Her language sometimes suggests that God's immanence is dissolved. I think that she can be defended against this claim although her language could possibly be refined at this point. As it is so often, it is not what she denies (if she does indeed deny it) which is important but what she is wanting to affirm—which is that just as the economic Trinity is about God's *soteriological* relationship *to the world*, so the immanent Trinity is about God's *communal* relationship *with persons*. 'The life of God—precisely because God is Triune—does not belong to God alone.'[29]

The divine life is also *our* life. The heart of the Christian life is to be united with the God of Jesus Christ by means of communion with one another. This is a *theosis*—union with God. The doctrine of the Trinity is not aimed at producing a theory of God's self-relatedness, it is about the encounter *between God and us*—a relational ontology.

So the Trinity is not primarily a statement about God's own life but a statement about God sharing life with us. It is, therefore, not helpful to describe the economic Trinity as a reference to God as God is revealed to us, and the immanent Trinity as a way of describing God *in se*. A theology of the immanent Trinity cannot refer to God apart from relationship to us but to God who is revealed in Christ and the Spirit. 'Trinitarian life is also our life.'[30] If we free ourselves from thinking that there are two levels to the Trinity (*ad intra* and *ad extra*) then we can see that there is one life of God in which we have graciously been included as partners. The doctrine of the Trinity is a teaching about God's life with us and our life with each other.

---

28 Wolfhart Pannenberg, *Systematic Theology*, Vol. 1 (Grand Rapids, Mich.: Eerdmans, 1988), 331.

29 LaCugna, *God for Us*, 1.
30 LaCugna, *God for Us*, 228.

The consummate Trinity unites a number of issues related to the economic and immanent dimensions of the Trinity. It takes one beyond soteriological thinking which is focused upon the individual to its proper end at the consummation and it also takes reflections on the inner relationships of God beyond a focus solely upon God in God's self to see God as a God who has taken up the cosmos into God's life. The Father is not only the Father of the Son, and the source of the Spirit, but now the Father of Glory, the one whose glory is revealed precisely at the consummation of all things. Glory was an immanent attribute of Yahweh sometimes revealed to humanity[31] but this inner glory of God shone out most brightly, and was revealed most clearly, in the life and work (economic) of Christ[32] but above all it is revealed at the Parousia, at the consummation of all things. The aim is that the whole world might know and glorify God.[33]

The practical implications of this cosmic consummation include the fact that the mission of the church includes caring for this world as best we are able. *Ecology* is a part of the church's mission. It also points emphatically towards the way that this is, primarily, God's mission. It is something that can be achieved only by God. It also points us towards *worship* as the ultimate focus of the church's mission.

This is the ultimate goal, and the unity, of evangelism and social justice. It is not that these activities do not have value in their own right but they are married together in looking forward eschatologically to the final kingdom of God where all exists in worship of God. This reminds us that even now any evangelism that does not lead people to an on-going life of worship within the church is not good evangelism; maybe it is not evangelism at all. And a mission which seeks peace and justice in this world which does not equally seek to bring about the peace of God (and not just the absence of war, discrimination and injustice) is not really mission either.

Perhaps most importantly of all, the present life of believers and the church will be enhanced with a deeper recognition of the significance of the consummate Trinity. Ostensibly trinitarian faith that is actually unitarian in practice inevitably lacks vitality. A recognition of the possibility of participation with God, that is, having a faith lived within the life of God, surrounded by and participating in the life of Jesus Christ and the Holy Spirit will come alive.

V Conclusion

Consequently the Trinity is the most profound part of the Christian faith. As it has been said, the Trinity is not a toy for theologians but a joy for believers. The Trinity is not the conclusion of a philosophical theology but the experience of actual Christian faith. Trinitarian doctrine is not, as some think, a philosophical, remote or removed doctrine. It is, in fact, the simplest, experientially lived and known doctrine.

John Wesley preached only one ser-

---

31 Exodus 16:7, 10; 24:15; 40:34-35; Lev. 9:6, 23.
32 Heb. 1:3; John1:14; 7:39; Luke 24:26; Acts 3:13; 8:55; Rom 6:4; 1 Tim. 3:16; 1 Peter 1:21.
33 Mark 8:38; 13:26; Rom. 15:9.

mon on the Trinity[34] but he thought consistently in a trinitarian way. It was, for him, not only a fundamental belief but also fundamental to a vital spiritual life. 'The knowledge of the Three-One God' he said, 'is interwoven with all true Christian faith; with all vital religion.' The individual believer may not explicitly recognise this, and may not use all the available theological terminology ('I do not mean that it is of importance to believe this or that explication of these words.') but it is essential *in practice* that the believer has the experience, 'the witness of the Spirit' that he is 'a child of God' who is 'accepted by the Father through the merits of the Son'.

The doctrine of the Trinity is primarily known by experiencing God as Father, Son and Spirit, rather than something comprehended by rational thought. There is, in fact, a paradox here, that we understand the Trinity most when we realize that we understand it only dimly. If we think that the doctrine of Trinity is entirely something of the mind and try to work it out along purely rational lines then we are altogether mistaken.

Fortunately, one of the most important aspects of this presentation of the consummate dimensions of the Trinity is that it actually tells us that *the life of God as Trinity is something in which we participate* rather than something to be intellectually comprehended. In effect it tells us that God cannot be fully known by reason but God can be fully loved.

---

34 John Wesley, *The Works of the Rev. John Wesley, MA, Sometime Fellow of Lincoln College, Oxford: With the Last Corrections of the Author* (London: Wesleyan-Methodist Book-Room, 1881), Sermon 55.

In the Name of the Father, Son, and Holy Spirit: Toward a Transcultural Trinitarian Worldview

J. Scott Horrell

Keywords: God, immanent and economic Trinity, human being, divine justice-forgiveness, Islam, global collaboration.

Broadly across Christian traditions today, the renaissance of Trinitarian studies continues to yield productive insights and needed correctives regarding the implications of faith in the tripersonal God. Some ideas align fairly readily with classical Christian faith, whereas others appear more distant from the Trinitarian creeds of Nicaea (325) and Constantinople (381) as historically interpreted. In primary terms, the doctrine of the Trinity affirms that the only true God eternally exists as three persons—Father, Son, and Holy Spirit—one in essence, united in glory, and distinct in relations.

On the one hand church fathers and present-day scholars alike admonish readers to beware of over-speculation regarding the Godhead, of trying to say too much about what cannot finally be said. The apophatic nature of Trinitarian confession indicates that creeds exist both to define the boundaries and to preserve the mystery of the transcendent God. As William Placher comments,

> We are asking about the very essence of God, and that essence is too great for our understanding. We must cling closely to Scripture and to the logic of salvation, flickering candles as it were against what seems such a great darkness but is in fact, of course, invisible to our mind's eyes because of the brilliance of its too great light.[1]

On the other hand, even as creedal language helps guard what can finally never be said, God has spoken in the Son and by the Spirit through acts in history and in the written word. The very centre of the biblical message is that the triune God comes to us and

---

1 William C. Placher, *The Triune God: An Essay in Postliberal Theology* (Louisville, KY: Westminster John Knox, 2007), 139.

J. Scott Horrell (ThM, ThD Dallas Theological Seminary) is Professor of Theological Studies at Dallas Theological Seminary. He serves as adjunct faculty at the Jordan Evangelical Theological Seminary (JETS, Amman), the Seminario Teológico CentroAmericano (SETECA, Guatemala), and the Centro de Desenvolvimento de Liderança (CDL) in Maputo, Mozambique. Half of the author's ministry life has been in Brazil and other countries of the world.

makes known his personal richness in mercy as well as judgment. We are invited to know this God through Christ and to be transformed by the renewing of our minds through the Word and by the Spirit. The theme of this article is that some things *can* be said about the Christian God in ways that may and should unite all believers.

This article proposes to outline a transcultural Trinitarian worldview that sets forth a universal framework of basic Christian faith for believers today. The different sections are meant as suggestions in the process of developing what it means for Christian believers to think about God and our human reality. I presuppose that the biblical basis and historical development of the doctrine of the Trinity are essentially and correctly expressed in the Niceno-Constantinopolitan Creed.[2] Yet the Creed should be understood both to contain the Trinitarian mystery and to open up within that framework fresh understandings among the nations of the world. Rather than a detailed discussion of any single aspect, this work is designed to be a rather simple synthesis of important Trinitarian themes.

The overview traces the Godhead's internal relationships from before creation, then discusses how Christians might think about God in relation to the physical universe, to themselves, and to others created in the image of God. In addition, the themes of divine love, holiness, and human redemption are briefly contrasted to non-Christian perspectives. In the penultimate section I posit several basic formulations about God, time, and space. The article concludes with two observations. Hence, these aspects of a theology of Trinity are designed to form a biblical-theological superstructure that unifies varying contextualized Christian perspectives of faith.

Integrated into the work is the conviction that the doctrine of the Holy Trinity with its broad-sweeping implications for human existence is a powerful apologetic for Christian faith amidst the cultures and belief systems of the world. Indeed, far from an embarrassment to avoid or a conundrum to try to explain, a biblical Trinitarian worldview is the most persuasive and truly beautiful invitation possible to believe in the Christian God.

Of course, any such framework calls for considerable humility before the mystery of God. Again, apophatic or negative theology—the theology of 'not-knowing'—surely has its place. Yet equally essential for a basic global Christian worldview is an open-handed working together among international believers in critiquing, correcting, and nuancing these kinds of ideas. Theology as Trinitarian worldview must arise from truly global dialogue with a chorus of voices.

I The Trinity before Creation

Tertullian wrote, 'Before all things God was alone, being his own universe, location, everything. He was alone, however, in the sense that there was nothing external to himself.'[3] Before

---

2 Commonly denominated the Nicene Creed, cf. Thomas C. Oden, ed., *Ancient Christian Doctrine*, 5 vols. (Downers Grove, IL: InterVarsity Press, 2009).

3 Tertullian, *Adversus Praxean*, 5.

any and all creation, it must be said that God was completely self-sufficient and all-inclusive. All that existed was God. There was nothing that was not God. Zwingli opined, 'Since we know that God is the source and creator of all things, we cannot conceive of anything before or beside him which is not also of him. For if anything could exist which was not of God, God would not be infinite.'[4] In the absolute beginning, God was everything.

This Supreme Being is infinite in each of his attributes. Rather than envelop *all* opposites as does the God of pantheism, the God of the Bible eternally exists in absolutely perfect nature of which nothing is greater. That is, God is pure and consistent in being—good and not evil, holy and not unholy, immutable and not ever-changing. And God is free. In one sense, God eternally chooses to be himself. He is what he is both by perfect nature and by choice.

The God who resides outside our dimensions cannot be exhaustively comprehended. He can be known in part yet he stands beyond us in mystery. Any true understanding we have of the transcendent God derives from God's gracious revelation given in finite categories and conditions that have meaning for us as finite beings. Nevertheless, what God has revealed of himself is authentic to who he is and wonderfully sufficient to know and to love him.

Moreover, the Supreme Being is profoundly personal. 'Though alone', before creation, Hippolytus remarks, 'he was multiple'.[5] God reveals himself as three eternally distinct persons. God is not fundamentally one God onto which a Trinity is added or flows forth. The absolute centre of God is Trinity.

Many in Christian tradition affirm that God as such has one mind, one will, and one activity. Others affirm that each person of the Godhead has distinct self-consciousness with mind, will, and actions in absolute harmony. In either case each member of the Godhead eternally indwells the other (termed *perichoresis*) without confusion of persons ('I am in the Father and the Father is in me' Jn. 14:11). In the mystery of the Trinity, the three persons coexist in unfathomable harmony in the one divine nature. Rather than some ethereal abstraction, the 'centre' of the Trinity is something like nuclear fusion.

The shared glory, love, and communication of the Father, the Son, and the Holy Spirit forever distinguish the Christian God from all other forms of theism. Thus, the persons of the Trinity can be known together as *one* yet also identified distinctly and worshipped.[6]

As the church fathers and the Nicene Creed affirm, the Father is the eternal Father of the eternal Son. Traditionally the Father is the unoriginate Origin, the Son is the eternal *only begotten* Son ('begotten but not made'), and the Holy Spirit eternally *proceeds*. As the Athanasian Creed would later articulate,

> So the Father is God, the Son God, and the Holy Spirit God; and yet not

---

4 Zwingli, 'An Exposition of the Faith', in *Zwingli and Bullinger*, ed. and trans. Geoffrey W. Bromiley (London: SCM Press, 1953), 249.

5 Hippolytus, *Contra Noetum*, 10.

6 See John Owen's *Communion with the Triune God*, ed. Kelly M. Kapic and Justin Taylor (Wheaton, IL: Crossway, 2007).

three Gods but one God. So the Father is Lord, the Son Lord, and the Holy Spirit Lord; and yet not three Lords but one Lord. For like as we are compelled by Christian truth to acknowledge every Person by himself to be both God and Lord; so are we forbidden by the catholic religion to say, there be three Gods or three Lords. The Father is made of none, neither created nor begotten. The Son is of the Father alone, not made nor created but begotten. The Holy Spirit is of the Father and the Son, not made nor created nor begotten but proceeding. So there is one Father not three Fathers, one Son not three Sons, and one Holy Spirit not three Holy Spirits. And in this Trinity there is nothing before or after, nothing greater or less, but the whole three Persons are coeternal together and coequal. So that in all things, as is aforesaid, the Trinity in Unity and the Unity in Trinity is to be worshipped.

The divine Being, before any and all creation, existed as all-inclusive, self-sufficient, and tripersonal in the high concept of Trinity.

II The Trinity and Impersonal Creation

Although a few people suppose a created order that is co-eternal in the past with God, classical Christian faith declares that creation has been called into existence out of nothing (*ex nihilo*). There was an absolute beginning. When God created, therefore, he deliberately chose to limit himself. While yet fully infinite, God now created something that was not himself.

In creating something out of absolute nothing, God no longer remained all-inclusive. The rock, the tree, and the zebra were not God. In contrast to all pantheistic theologies, the God of the Bible did not flow or emanate out into the physical world. On the contrary, all space, energy, and matter exist as God's creation and artistry and not as his essence. Nevertheless, the existence of these dimensions is wholly sustained by the personal Creator. As Thomas Finger observes, as radical as it may be,

The Trinitarian God remains distinctly *other*. God's intertwining with creatures thus evokes heightened wonder, for it proceeds not from natural necessity—not because we already are God's body—but from grace.[7]

Apart from sin, all creation is centripetal to God's character. The triune God himself is the centre of everything. Bonaventure believed in the actual presence of the Trinity in the universe: 'The created world is like a book in which its Maker, the Trinity, shines forth, is represented, and can be read...'[8] Richard Foster comments, 'God loves matter. In his original creative acts God affirmed matter again and again, declaring it good at every point along the way. We, therefore, should take the material world quite seriously.'[9]

Whether three-leaf clovers, identical triplets, or the three subatomic

---

[7] Thomas Finger, 'Modern Alienation and Trinitarian Creation', *Evangelical Review of Theology* 17:2 (April 1993), 204.
[8] Bonaventure, *Breviloquium*, 2, 12.
[9] Richard J. Foster, *Streams of Living Water* (HarperSanFrancisco, 1998), 260.

quarks that form the protons and neutrons of the universe—and a thousand other Trinitarian analogies—all creation reflects something of the Creator. Yet all illustrations fall short.

The question of *why* God created is not easily answered, although classical Christian faith responds in the final sense 'to the praise of his glory' (Eph. 1:12-13). Many surmise that the divine motivation for creation is best found in the overflow of loving self-givingness between the three persons of the Godhead. The deep love and joyful relations among the members of the Trinity are manifested in the creation of that which is *other* than God—especially other personal beings that might know and enjoy relationship, service, and worship of this God.

Summarily, the triune God brought the created order into existence out of nothing. He sustains it and in that sense is personally related to all dimensions of existence. Yet God is not to be confused with that which he created and sustains.

III The Trinity and the Unity-Diversity of the Universe

The tension between the unity and diversity of the universe is one of the great philosophic problems of history. Since the ancient philosophers, humanity has lacked a solution to this enigma. Is reality constituted by a single cosmic principle that determines all existence (Fate or God)? That is, is the universe an absolute *one*? Or is the universe an absolute *many*? Is ultimate reality located in a diversity in which the particulars are random or free (whether by chance or by choice)?

At the pole of unity, one is locked in cosmic determinism. Whether religious or secular, I am but a tiny cog within a massive machine over which I have no control and in which I have no basis for choice or personal meaning. Such a perspective is evident in the religious fatalism of ancient Greek religions, or the passivism of Advaita Vedanta, traditional Islam (*inshallah* 'If-God-wills'), and extreme Christian predestinationism.

The problem becomes even worse in scientific naturalism. All activities reduce to necessity—whether in Marxism's dialectic materialism, contemporary neurobiology, or behavioural psychology. A human being is reduced to one's DNA of evolutionary survival and to variations of social conditioning. The concept of *person* is merely a ghost in the machine. Neither religious nor secular fatalism yields a meaningful place for the individual.

At the opposite pole, that of diversity, all existence is composed of particulars with no ultimate unifying Being or *telos*. Such religions picture humanity coping within a chaos of cosmic flux or a myriad of forces and spirits. In western atheism, 'We make ourselves'. 'I am the centre of the universe.' The spirit of the Enlightenment is that 'Without God I am free!'

But what is freedom with no referent beyond oneself? I might be *free*. But in an empty universe such freedom would be like floating in outer space with neither spacecraft nor planet in sight and only two hours of oxygen before I die. Freedom itself is meaningless. From Kandinsky and Dadaism to Basquiat, Cy Twombly, and Cindy Sherman, twentieth-century art reveals the angst of being one's own god in a meaningless universe.

Outside of biblical Christianity, there is no structure that finally satisfies the tension between the one and the many. As three persons in one God, the Trinity incorporates both unity and diversity within itself. Apart from direct revelation, explains Cornelius Van Til, we could never know that God exists tripersonally. But that being revealed, we surely can understand 'that the unity and the plurality of this world has [in] back of it a God in whom unity and the plurality are equally ultimate'.[10] Creation reflects this unity-diversity from the immensity of outer space with its at least two hundred billion galaxies, to the complexity of inner space with sub-atomic quarks, leptons, and bosons. Whether vastly expansive or fathomlessly small, there is order between individual components and the total scheme of creation.

In the end, as often expressed, if there is no infinite, absolute point of reference in the universe, then all of the particulars are meaningless. What is more, if such a point of reference is to give real significance to all existence, it must be a personal Absolute, a 'Thou'. In contrast with all other religions and philosophies, the concept of the Holy Trinity presents a meaningful relationship between the one and the many in the universe. Every thing and every person has real significance because they were created by and exist related to the triune God. Even if a person does not believe in God, in fact, his or her existence is of immense value because God has created them for himself.

---

10 Cornelius Van Til, *An Introduction to Systematic Theology*, ed. William Edgar (2d ed., Phillipsburg, NJ: P & R, 2007), 364-65.

IV The Trinity and the Beginning of Personal Creation

Besides space, time and matter, the triune God chose to create other *persons*. By creating self-conscious beings God limited himself again. No longer was God the only moral and spiritual agent in existence. Unlike God himself, all created beings are finite, whether in heaven or on earth. In contrast to God the Son, for example, Satan is not capable of being present in all places at all times; rather he extends his kingdom through his minions. In creating finite persons, the God of the Bible remains infinite but he is no longer morally and volitionally all-inclusive; now a personal being could choose against him.

Contrary to the atheist and the pantheist, the Judeo-Christian affirms that human personhood and dignity is grounded in the *imago Dei*. While more ample than these aspects, *personhood* surely includes the simple elements of thought, volition, and emotion: (1) God thinks and reasons in a logical manner, although not necessarily in the same thought patterns that we use; (2) God chooses voluntarily and possesses freedom of will; and (3) God manifests a multiplicity of affections—all as a moral, purposeful Being.

Just as Scripture establishes that each member of the Godhead reasons, exercises volition, and manifests a plurality of feelings, so we as finite persons evince similar characteristics. Other aspects of the divine image appear to include creativity, aesthetic appreciation, moral conscience, aptitude for dominion, a sense of immortality, and the desire and capacity for I-thou relationships.

Therefore, although human beings have fallen into sin and suffer the defects of the fall, the *imago Dei* is not disfigured beyond recognition. We are truly persons with eternal value because the Creator and Absolute of the universe is also personal. And God has come to us in Jesus Christ, the express image and manifestation of God.

In sum, Trinitarianism argues that neither atheism nor pantheism has a sufficient framework for explaining our humanness—the full-bodied 'humanness' presumed worldwide through literature, music, and common life. Nor does Islam teach that human beings are created in the image of God; rather it says we are creatures made to serve but not to fellowship with Allah.

In Christianity, the doctrine of God as Father, Son, and Holy Spirit is the structure and ontological grounding for the realities of our own personhood: our self-consciousness, rationality (including language), self-determinative choices, plethora of affections and emotions, sense of afterlife, moral sensibilities of right and wrong, capacity for dominion over the earth, and our desire for relationships with God and with other human beings. Of course the infinite God transcends our realities, therefore our parallels must be understood by analogy. Yet in Trinitarian faith, our humanity has found its home.

V The Trinity and Humanity in Community

The doctrine of the Trinity yields further light for the individual in social relationships. From eternity past, the Father, Son, and Holy Spirit unite in communication, fellowship, and love, thus in a plenitude of interpersonal relationships.[11] In the secular world, many declare that human relationships exist only to serve our selfish interests, that 'love' is simply the product of biological hormones, and that language is a tool of manipulation. No longer are such attitudes merely oriented to the North Atlantic. From Beijing to Buenos Aires many find life without significance. The words of Bob Dylan bemoan the hopelessness of a tired, adult humanity, 'I used to care, but things have changed.'[12]

In the midst of anti-humanitarian affirmations, the Christian faith proclaims that communication, friendship, and love—all central human desires—assume profound meaning when we understand that humankind was created by a Godhead that manifests social relations within itself. From conception and birth, to language and cultural formation, to values acquisition, to our physical daily wellbeing (if not survival), we are dependent upon social relations.

We are created for community. Whereas God as Trinity is self-sufficient, we are not. Created as individuals, we are made, so to speak, for a trinity of relationships—with self, other human beings, and the Lord God. As creatures rather than Creator, we are not designed to presume ourselves all-knowing, to attain ultimate perspective, or to be in the centre of our

---

[11] For biblical evidence, see Horrell, 'The Eternal Son of God in the Social Trinity', *Jesus in Trinitarian Perspective: An Introductory Christology*, ed. Fred Sanders and Klaus Issler, (Nashville, TN: B & H Academic, 2007), 44-79.

[12] Bob Dylan, from the song "Things Have Changed", *Modern Times*, Sony, 2006.

universe. A person is designed to trust in and to enter into fellowship with the triune God.

If the one God is three persons in relationship and if I am created to reflect or *image* my Maker, then I have every reason to enter into full human relations: to work with others for the good of all; to engage in reasoned thought and communication; to enjoy objective study of science, history, and other disciplines of learning; to create and participate within the visual arts and music; to express emotions of joy, sadness, and anger in my personal associations; to pursue and develop friendships in healthy, appropriate ways; to value social connections around the births, marriages, anniversaries, and deaths of others; to delight in sexual intimacy in marriage (which reflects the covenantal nature of God's own unity, hence to be guarded as sacred); to be zealous for justice and compassion among those laden by poverty, oppression, hardship, and sin; to care for our earth over which we remain viceregents.

This is not to deny a fallen world with the surd that separates and destroys believers and unbelievers alike. Rather it is to say that as Christians we have a structure for being persons-in-relation in the world and, all the more, in the context of the believing community, the church.

Thus the Christian faith leads us to the depths of our humanity. Made in God's likeness, now forgiven and reborn, the more we become like Jesus Christ (the perfect *imago Dei*) the more we reflect the wondrous personal glory of God. True Christianity does not erase the person, nor is it careless toward community—in contrast to many forms of pantheism and atheism. On the contrary, biblical faith leads the Christian to full personhood in relationship with others. No human being in all of history compares to Jesus of Nazareth in his purity, magnetism, and profound relations with others. That which we see in the humanity of the Last Adam corresponds to the ontology of every human being, an ontology that is awakened and renewed through faith in the Saviour.

VI The Trinity and Love, Justice, and Forgiveness

Two central characteristics of the God of the Bible are justice and love. Beginning with the latter, love is beautifully manifest in the relationship between the Father and the Son (Jn. 17:23-24), and further in God's sacrificial love for the world (1 Jn. 4:7-10). Defined in 1 Corinthians 13, *agape* is not directed inwardly but outwardly in the sharing and giving of oneself to others. In contrast to Islam, Judaism, and other religions that insist God exists exclusively as one person, the triune God of Christianity is not egocentric, solitary, or isolated.

Richard of St. Victor wrote,

> It is never said of anyone that he possesses charity because of the exclusively personal love that he has for himself—for there to be charity, there must be a love that is directed towards another. Consequently where there is an absence of a plurality of persons, there cannot be charity.[13]

---

13 Richard of St. Victor, *De Trinitate*, 1.20.

Richard further argued that the delight of shared love, as supreme happiness, involves not just two persons but three. The tripersonal God does not need to create something or someone to love. God is love in its resplendent fullness apart from creation. Yet he invites created persons into the divine fellowship through faith in the Son.

As Jesus Christ revealed God to the world, so he taught us to follow him by way of the cross (Lk. 9:23-25). By the giving of ourselves in love to others we are transformed into godlikeness, the *imago Dei*. A fundamental principle for being human is that the more we strive to give of ourselves, first to God and then to others, the more fulfilled we are as personal beings.

In sacrificially loving others, we imitate the persons of the Trinity—the Father as he gives 'all things' to the Son (Jn. 16:15; 17:10), the Son as he obeys the Father (Jn. 5:30; 8:29; Phil. 2:8) and when having conquered all he gives 'all things' back to the Father (1 Cor. 15:27-28), and the Spirit as he selflessly glorifies the Son and the Father (Jn. 16:13-15).

This divine self-givingness within God's personal plurality serves as our model, first in our response to God himself, but secondarily in our social relationships, whether in the family, local church, or at any other sociological level.

Just as God is love, so he is holy and just. The only attribute thrice repeated in both Testaments is the trisagion, the seraphs' cry of 'Holy, holy, holy is the Lord [God] Almighty' (Is. 6:3; cf. Rev. 4:8). Some thirty times in Isaiah alone God is the 'Holy One', he who is other, mysterious, and perfect. Jesus is called the same in the New Testament (Mk. 1:24; Jn. 6:69; Rev. 3:7) One aspect of God's holiness is his justice. God is the absolute moral standard of all existence; all right and wrong are directly related to his moral purity and role as the Holy One and Judge.

How can God's holy justice coexist with God's love if sin should enter the world? If God were unipersonal he could be perfectly just and holy, but he would be equally unable to forgive sin without violating his own justice. In Islam's Hadith (the sayings of Muhammad), Allah stands above the bridge that passes from this earthly life to the afterlife of paradise. Underneath this bridge 'as narrow as the edge of a sword' is the burning abyss of hell.[14] Every Muslim admits that he is not morally perfect as Allah is perfect; he can only cast himself on divine mercy.

But in Islam there can be no certainty of God's mercy. Allah does whatever he chooses. All Muslims believe God forgives, but the question is how? A person who lives a life ninety percent good and ten percent evil might be granted paradise. A person with less virtue might be pushed into the abyss. But no one knows what Allah will do. The point is this: assuming that no one is perfect as God is perfect, Allah must compromise his justice in order to forgive so that some enter Paradise. Yet if Allah compromises his justice he is no longer the Moral Absolute of the universe.

Conversely, the New Testament declares that God is both the Just and Justifier of those who have faith in Jesus (Rom. 3:23-26). In that 'all have

---

14 Sura 19:68-71, 'The Bridge Sirat', from which the Hadith analogy is developed.

sinned and fall short of the glory of God', neither works of the law nor acts of righteousness remove our judgment. Rather, precisely because God is more than one person, this God can both demand absolute justice and he himself pay the price that he requires. Because of the plurality of persons, the triune God can be the Holy Judge, the sacrificial Lamb who satisfies divine justice, and the sanctifying Spirit who works within me (even when a sinner) to lead me to God and to make me his child. Because the God of the Bible is Trinity, he is 'big' enough to be both perfectly just and perfectly forgiving to all who trust in the Son.

VII The Trinity and Time and Space

In forming a transcultural Trinitarian worldview, the most speculative realm is that of God in relation to time and space. Yet certain tentative observations can be set forth that reflect historical Christian thought.

Unlike the cyclical concept of time in classical pantheism and some forms of animism, the biblical perspective of time is linear: the history of the world has beginning, direction, and culmination. For this reason, more than any other religion, Judeo-Christianity has large numbers of predictive prophecies—by one well-known estimate over a quarter of the Bible.[15] The Christian faith takes objective history seriously as demonstrated in the incarnation, ministry, death, resurrection, and second coming of Jesus Christ (*cf.* 1 Cor. 15:3-27). God enters creational time and space dynamically relating with human beings. Simultaneously this same sovereign God is transcendent, existing outside and beyond his creation.

Seen from a biblical viewpoint, time and creation have a beginning but they have no end. The physical order was created and will continue in *some form* forever, although the nature of time and space may be radically transformed. Such fundamental categories of existence belong to the covenant that the triune God has made with finite beings. Believers are given 'eternal life'—a life filled with the plenitude of the Lord, a life of elevated quality, finally with 'spiritual bodies' (1 Cor. 15:44)—but always within some form of time and space whether heavenly or earthly (Rev. 22:2), as these seem essential to the existence of finite beings.

Furthermore, in Christian tradition God the Son has forever assumed a human nature (body and soul, Jn. 1:14), although that in no way confines his deity. The Holy Spirit, likewise, is manifested as a dove and tongues of fire. If not merely metaphorical, some language of Scripture suggests that even God the Father appears in finite forms within the orders of creation (*i.e.*, the Ancient of Days, Dan. 7:9-10). Indeed, certain concepts of heaven include some kind of appearance of the Father ('him who sits on the throne', Rev. 4:9,10) while mainline theological understandings affirm him as exclusively immortal, invisible, 'whom no one has seen or can see' (1 Tim. 6:15).

However conceived, by God's entering the world—principally in the Incar-

---

15 J. Barton Payne, *Encyclopedia of Biblical Prophecy: The Complete Guide to Scriptural Predictions and Their Fulfillment* (Grand Rapids, MI: Baker, 1973), 681, puts the figure at 27 percent.

nation of the Son and by the ever-active Spirit—we can understand and relate to God in tangible ways. Indeed, if the infinite God did *not* reveal himself in words and appearances analogous to human reality, then we would be without categories to understand and relate to him. Whenever God reveals himself it is by grace and condescension.

From this vantage, the triune God reveals himself through finite forms without limiting himself to those forms. He is simultaneously inside and outside creation, not bound to but active within the created orders. In this way, the Trinity's presence encompasses both creation and non-creation, preserving divine transcendent autonomy (termed the *immanent* Trinity) together with the Godhead's functional working within creation (the *economic* Trinity).

People often think in two dimensions: heaven and earth. But it may be better to conceive of reality in at least three spheres in respect to God: (1) our universe and the world in which the triune God has shown himself, most properly in the Incarnation; (2) the celestial dimension of angels where saints too will have glorified bodies before the eternal God-man Jesus Christ and in the presence of the Father; and (3) the transcendent, immanent Trinity, beyond all dimensions and ultimately all comprehension.

Conclusion: The Trinity, Glory, and Christendom Today

In view of the infinite, personal nature of the Most High God as revealed in the Bible with absolute perfection, self-sufficiency, unchangeableness, and free will, and in view of the Trinitarian structure of the universe which gives meaning to human beings as persons—with rationality, morality, love, balance between unity and diversity, and so very much more—something yet needs to be said. Nearly everything mentioned until now is related to *our* worldview, our human perspective. However, having begun with the Trinity before creation, we pause to realize that everything that is not creation is God.

If the tripersonal God existed as the all-inclusive One before creation, then surrounding creation (and sustaining creation) resides the infinite triune Lord, the Lord of all, exercising his magnificent character. For those who are Christians, redeemed by the work of Christ at the cross, finite creation constitutes an enormous 'crib' over which and around which the triune God hovers, affectionately caring for his own. All creation will someday recognize the greatness and beauty of God, together with the unfathomable debt it owes to the Almighty for its existence and preservation, and for the provision of salvation in Christ Jesus.

It is likely that this overwhelming understanding of our utter indebtedness to God is our main role as created personal beings. In glorifying the Father, the Son, and the Holy Spirit we are fulfilled as finite persons in the eternal plan of God. Nonetheless, there is no more blessed glory than that glory given by each member of the Trinity to the other, each wholly comprehending and exalting the greatness of the other.

The First Ecumenical Council of Nicaea (325) and its theological development at Constantinople (381) established the confessional centre of Christian faith. We began our overview with a warning to respect divine mystery, reminding ourselves that there is much we do not know and much more about which we have only opinions, given the ambiguity of biblical and historical evidence. Yet the Niceno-Constantinopolitan Creed frames the boundaries of what is licit versus what must not be said.

Within this confession we should welcome new cultural constructions of Trinitarian doctrine as believers worldwide seek to articulate more deeply the Christian doctrine of God and its meaning for their lives and cultures. Surely some of the miss-steps that yet plague wider expressions of Christendom will reoccur (and these must be deemed in error). Yet as Christianity's masses increasingly and overwhelmingly weigh the scales to the global South, believers with non-western languages and thought forms should endeavour to articulate Trinitarian doctrine and to work out its implications for how they should live in the midst of their own changing milieus.

The purpose of this article has been to offer a tentative framework for a transcultural Trinitarian worldview. The biblical-theological superstructure suggested here can help unify varying contextualized expressions of Christian faith around Trinitarian confession. Of course, the international reader will rightly complain that the author's perspective is largely western and North Atlantic. For this reason believers in different cultures need one another—to challenge, enlarge, deepen, and balance varying perspectives. But the suggestion, humbly submitted, is especially for a missional Trinitarian worldview—not missional as from one culture to another, but missional as each body of believers seeks to engage and express Trinitarian faith within its own culture.

Believers are to live out the faith they profess. And so, in the plurality and beauty of the body of Christ worldwide, may the understanding of the triune God continue to unfold in fresh insights and intentional application—in the name of the Father, the Son, and the Holy Spirit. John of Damascus lends an eloquent doxology: 'O Father! O coequal Son! O coeternal Spirit! In Persons Three, in Substance One, and One in power and merit; in Thee baptiz'd, we Thee adore for ever and for evermore!'[16]

---

[16] John of Damascus, 'Canon for Easter Day, called the Queen of Canons', Ode VIII. 'Thou hallowed chosen morn of praise', in *Hymns of the Eastern Church*, ed. and trans., J. M. Neale, 3rd ed. (London: J. T. Hayes, 1870), 106.

The Trinity and Servant-Leadership

William P. Atkinson

Keywords: Egalitarianism, exaltation, image, kenosis, leadership, Pentecost, servant

As the title of my article suggests, I will be reflecting on what resources consideration of the Trinity offers for the exercise of leadership by trinitarians, whether that leadership be in the church or in wider society. In contrast to impressions given in some recent delineations of the matter, I will be concluding that strong leadership is neither inherently destructive and abusive nor needing to be replaced by 'flat' egalitarianism. Rather, it is to be found in the Trinity, in a form that is protected from autocracy by the self-emptying, or 'kenosis' of the one who is leading. As such, it can be mirrored in human life, so long as the leadership in question is genuinely servant-leadership. This form of leadership is freeing for the people who are being led, and effective in achieving the purposes of the organisation being led.

To those who are familiar with various shades of trinitarianism, it will be obvious from the outset that the particular form of trinitarianism that is most easily applicable to servant-leadership is a 'social' form. This article proceeds to work within the framework of social trinitarianism. It is also obvious to students of trinitarianism that social trinitarianism highlights three-ness in God. Its defence of oneness in God is sometimes weaker, and proponents of social trinitarianism have occasionally been accused of straying rather too close to tritheism for comfort. I do not seek to engage with that discussion in this article. Suffice it to say that I believe in one God, and regard perichoresis as the best defence of God's unity.

I Applying One's Trinitarianism

As this article is a contribution to a journal number dedicated to considering 'applied trinitarianism', I take it as read that in some way the Trinity is applicable to the human sphere, and that I do not need here to defend such a stance. I do, however, think that care needs to be taken in thinking about the lines along which this application can be pursued. Some sort of relation

---

Rev Dr William P. Atkinson (MA, London Bible College; PhD, University of Edinburgh) is Director of Research and Senior Lecturer in Pentecostal and Charismatic Studies at the London School of Theology. He was for some years Principal of Regents Theological College, the denominational training centre of the Elim Pentecostal Churches, with which he is ordained. He has also served in pastoral ministry in several local congregations. He is author of The 'Spiritual Death' of Jesus *(Brill, 2009),* Baptism in the Spirit *(Pickwick, 2011), and* Trinity After Pentecost *(Pickwick, 2013).*

between divine being and human being must be posited as a basis for any sort of analogical thinking that draws conclusions for humanity from the divine being.

Typically at this point, a relation of similarity is sought, so that a conclusion can be reached that 'as God is, so is humanity', or 'as God is, so ought to be humanity'. It is often sought in one particular strand of biblical thinking about the divine creation of humans. The account in Genesis 1 provides data for this pursuit. Humans are made in the divine image and likeness (Gen. 1:26-27), and as such no doubt reflect certain divine characteristics. A clear example of this starting point at work is to be found pervading Tom Smail's *Like Father, Like Son*, which is tellingly subtitled, *The Trinity Imaged in Our Humanity*, and which, perhaps even more tellingly, has chapter titles which all include the word, 'Image'.[1]

This approach is potentially problematic, however. First, it offers no guidance as to what *aspects* of human being are in God's image. Is human physicality, for instance, divinely imaged? Are we to infer that God has two eyes? Secondly, it does not clarify *extent*: how closely human being mirrors the divine. Assuredly, Genesis may well have been intended to indicate that the first humans reflected something of God's being in their own. However, and regarding the early chapters of Genesis as a narrative with inner coherence, these first humans were persuaded by the serpent to eat something that would enable them to 'be like God' (Gen. 3:5, NIV). So they were not 'like God' entirely. Where, then, lay the limits of their Godlikeness?

Thirdly, *chronology* is unclear: still granting these chapters of Genesis narrative coherence, these first two humans gave in to the serpent's persuasion and behaved in a way that led to dire consequences. Now, certain curses pertained. If these humans had been in God's image before this 'fall' from their pristine state, who is to say to what degree this divine image remained intact thereafter? As later scriptures in the canon remain relatively quiet on this point, Christians have expressed ongoing uncertainty through continued debate.

Thus no firm conclusion can be reached for humanity by gazing reverently at the Trinity and declaring, 'on the basis of the divine image at creation, as God is, so are we'. I seek a different starting point, not in creation but in redemption, not in a statement concerning how humans were, but in a wish concerning what they might come to be. I begin, in fact, with Christ's 'high-priestly' prayer presented in John 17, which I believe gives us an opportunity to state, 'on the basis of this prayer, as God is, so God wishes us to be'.

What I find here, among other requests, is the wish expressed that certain qualities of relationship between humans might reflect the quality of relationship between the Father and the Son that Jesus knew existed (for such is the import of the prayer's wording). In particular, Jesus prayed for those the Father had given him, that 'they may be one as we are one' (Jn. 17:11, NIV), and for later believers that they may be one 'just as you are in me and

---

[1] Tom Smail, *Like Father, Like Son: The Trinity Imaged in Our Humanity* (Grand Rapids, MI; Cambridge: Eerdmans, 2005).

I am in you . . . I in them and you in me' (Jn. 17:21, 23, NIV). This 'in-ness' of one person in another is later expressed in terms of love: '. . . in order that the love you have for me may be in them and that I myself may be in them' (Jn. 17:26).

It will be obvious to those with even a smattering of New Testament Greek that 'in' here could just as well be translated 'among'. This fits with the request for Jesus' disciples to be 'one'. The prayer is not for Christ's followers as isolated individuals, but for them as a community.

Of course, one of the doubts about the divine image referred to in Genesis 1 must also be acknowledged here: that of *extent*. I noted that the divine image did not protect Eve from the serpent's temptation for her to do that which would make her 'like God', indicating in the logic of the narrative that there were differences as well as similarities between the divine and the human. So too in John 17 no indication is given about where the boundaries lie between the sort of unity that Christ's followers can experience with one another and the sort of unity that the Father and the Son enjoy.

However, the other two weaknesses concerning the Genesis 1 reference to divine image are overcome. Now, the *aspect* is clear. It is loving relationship. The reference to love indicates a quality of relationship that is to flow from that between the Father and the Son into the created realm, between Christ's followers. As there is love between the Father and the Son, so there is to be love between Christians—and indeed the same sort of love—'in-one-another-type-love'—as between Father and Son. There is to be, so to speak, a divine overflow of love.

Also, *chronology* is somewhat clearer: this is a future quality to which Jesus looks forward. It is something we can confidently hope for and work for. (I admit, however, that it is still unclear how far this prayer can be answered in this life; presumably, it can fully be answered only in the resurrection life to come—Jn. 11:25, etc.)

I conclude from this presentation of the Johannine Jesus' prayer that an important NT strand of thinking, expressed more subtly elsewhere, is that there is available to humans, in and through their relationship with God in Christ, a loving quality of their relationships with each other that reflects the quality of divine love within the Trinity. This is my starting point for exploring the 'application' of trinitarianism to matters of human relatedness, including in the case of this article the matter of servant-leadership.

I will be arguing that the Trinity can be conceived in a way that, on the basis of the divine-human connection set out above, means that Jesus' high-priestly prayer is, among many other things, a plea for servant-leadership within the church. I will thus be disagreeing with calls for 'flat' egalitarian relationships in church life and other social structures. I will also, of course, be disagreeing with views of the Trinity that see the divine relations as symmetrically egalitarian and 'flat'. I will be seeing leadership within the Trinity (unsurprisingly centred in the Father), but will be seeing this as servant-leadership. The link between service and leadership will be the link of self-emptying love. We call this self-emptying 'kenosis'.

II Kenosis and Exaltation

There are many ways that the love between the trinitarian persons can be explored. In my recent book, *Trinity After Pentecost*,[2] I explored the Trinity from the point of view of Pentecost, as is natural from my own Pentecostal perspective. In particular, I looked at what the events of Pentecost meant for the divine persons. This led me to consider kenosis and exaltation, as I will set out in this section.

A word, first, about my methods: as soon as one begins to look at the Trinity by way of events in salvation-history, whether one chooses Pentecost,[3] the cross,[4] the incarnation,[5] the conception,[6] or any other such event, one is inevitably glimpsing the triune God as this God expresses the divine self through these events—through the 'economy' of world-history and especially salvation-history. This so-called 'economic Trinity' is all we have to look at, for the portals of heaven remain as yet otherwise unopened.

We trust that God's self-revealing honesty ensures that, while far more may be true of the 'immanent Trinity'—what God is in the eternal divine self—than can be known from the 'economic Trinity', nevertheless what the activities of the divine persons reveal of God's self is true of God's eternal 'inner' self. If this were not so, we could know nothing of God's nature through what has happened in our world.

One other brief methodological point I will make is that the choice to focus on Pentecost puts me firmly in Lukan territory (I take it as established that the same author wrote the third gospel and the Acts of the Apostles). Nevertheless, the whole NT witnesses to a decisive eruption of the activity of the Spirit of God among God's people in, through, and after the earthly ministry of Jesus Christ. Pentecost came, according to all the NT witnesses—whatever they called it and whatever weight they would have put on Luke's precise details of an upper room, a vast pilgrim crowd, excited speaking in tongues, and mass conversion.

Pentecost came, in the sense that the Spirit was now experienced as a reality for all the new covenant people of God in Christ, rather than a select few (Joel 2:28; cf. Acts 2:17). Pentecost came, in the sense that the Spirit previously experienced as the Spirit of God was now, also, experienced as the Spirit of Christ, whether that primarily meant that the Spirit conveyed the felt presence of Christ (especially in Paul), or it meant primarily that the ascended and exalted Christ sent the Spirit—from the Father (especially in Luke-Acts), or both (especially in John). My discussion does not just have to do with some sort of skewed 'Lukan' Trinity or trinitarianism.

I was first encouraged to try glimpsing the Trinity from the viewpoint of

---

[2] William P. Atkinson, *Trinity After Pentecost* (Eugene, OR: Pickwick, 2013).

[3] So, as well as here, Steve M. Studebaker, *From Pentecost to the Triune God* (Grand Rapids, MI; Cambridge: Eerdmans, 2012).

[4] So Jürgen Moltmann, *The Crucified God* (English Translation; London: SCM, 1974 [1973]).

[5] So Karl Rahner, *The Trinity* (English Translation; London; New York: Continuum, 1970 [1967]).

[6] So Tom Smail, *The Giving Gift*. (London: Hodder and Stoughton, 1988). Although this is a work of pneumatology, it is set in a firmly trinitarian framework.

Pentecost by Max Turner. His impetus is clear from the following chapter title of his: 'Towards Trinitarian Theology—Perspectives from Pentecost'.[7] His references to Acts 2:33 intrigued me. While he sees in this text an implicit distinction between the Father and the Spirit (for otherwise Jesus would be sending the Father—an idea that Turner regards as blasphemous), his primary interest is in the implications this statement has for Lukan divine christology (only God can send God's Spirit; Jesus sends God's Spirit: therefore, Jesus is divine). It was, in this regard, his strongly worded reference to Jesus' now being, in effect, 'Lord' of the Spirit that especially caught my attention.[8]

While Turner thought through the implications of this in terms of the exaltation of Christ, I thought it through in terms of the humility of the Spirit. According to Luke, in Jesus' life on earth, the Spirit had led Jesus (e.g., Lk. 4:1) and been the source of his joy (Lk. 10:21). Jesus had thus been dependent, at least in some respects, on the resources of the Spirit. After Christ's ascension, however, Jesus was now 'in charge of' the Spirit, so to speak, sending the Spirit to earth. In some regards, roles had reversed.[9] I saw in this a humble 'kenosis', or self-emptying, of the Spirit: the person of the Spirit was prepared in humility to take a subservient role in relation to Christ, having tasted a leading role.

The idea of a kenosis of the Spirit may surprise some. We are used to the idea, however it has been expressed, of the kenosis of the Son. The pre-incarnate Son did not keep a tight grip on heavenly glory but was willing to undergo a self emptying, or 'kenosis', thereby suffering the degradations and deprivations of earthly life. In the NT, the most direct testimony to this idea is the well-known hymn in Philippians 2, where in verse 7 the term, in verb form, is used. As the NRSV translates it, Christ 'emptied himself'. The idea can be understood not only with respect to the created order but also with respect to the Son's relations with the Father. The Son emptied himself not just, or even primarily, for the salvation of humanity, but for the sake of the Father and the Father's glory (e.g., Phil. 2:11).

Can this idea of kenosis apply to other persons of the Trinity? Yes. When we turn our gaze to Pentecost, most particularly but not exclusively as this event was presented in Acts, we can see a kenosis of the Spirit in two regards. We can see one, first, with respect to the created order (the Spirit, admittedly did not undergo temptation, hunger, etc. as the Son did; however, the Spirit at Pentecost humbly entered feeble, fallible human hearts). Secondly, as I introduced above, the Spirit underwent kenosis with respect to the Son (the Spirit who had led the Son in the latter's earthly ministry was now willing to be sent by that same—now exalted—Son).

If we look closely, we can also see a dynamic reciprocation between kenosis and exaltation. The humble, self-

---

[7] Chapter 11 of Max Turner, *The Holy Spirit and Spiritual Gifts: Then and Now* (Carlisle: Paternoster, 1996).

[8] Turner, *Holy Spirit and Spiritual Gifts*, 174.

[9] Jürgen Moltmann, in a somewhat different context, makes the same point (*Trinity and Kingdom* [English Translation; Minneapolis: Fortress Press, 1993 (1980)], 89; cf. 211).

emptied, kenotic Son exalted the Spirit in his earthly ministry (Lk. 4:18; 11:20; 12:12; 24:49);[10] but in turn it was as a result of the Son's own kenosis that he was later exalted. Now, this exalted Son sent the Spirit, and in turn the kenotic, sent Spirit of Pentecost exalted the Son, through the Christ-extolling preaching of the Spirit-empowered church. By way of analogy, this temporal dynamic reciprocation, I suggest, reflects an eternal dynamic reciprocation between the Son and the Spirit in which each empties self in order to exalt the other, and in which the kenosis of the self is rewarded by exaltation.

As interesting as the kenosis of the Spirit and the Son are to trinitarianism, the intra-trinitarian kenosis that is of most interest to this article's focus is that of the Father. If the idea of the Spirit's kenosis is somewhat surprising, a posited kenosis of the Father is perhaps even more counter-intuitive. Surely, one might think, of all the persons of the Trinity, the Father at least abides in eternal exaltation, 'uncomplicated' by kenosis of any sort? To those who think thus, I say, 'Think again!' Amidst the reciprocal dynamics of kenosis and exaltation between Son and Spirit, the Father does not remain aloof from such vicissitudes as the untouchable, unimpassioned, only-exalted Ultimate.

When Moltmann looked at the Trinity from the nearby viewpoint of the cross, he rightly saw the self-emptying and suffering of the Father in that event.[11] The cross was not only a self-emptying act of selfless love expressed by the Son. The Father, in giving the Son, gave of the divine fabric of his own being. The Father emptied himself in love. In this event, among other agonies, a 'sword pierced the Father's soul too' (cf. Lk. 2:35, NIV). As Moltmann writes elsewhere:

> If the Father forsakes the Son, the Son does not merely lose his sonship. The Father loses his fatherhood as well. The love that binds the one to the other is transformed into a dividing curse. It is only as the One who is forsaken and cursed that the Son is still the Son. It is only as the One who forsakes, who surrenders the other, that the Father is still present. Communicating love and responding love are alike transformed into infinite pain and into the suffering and endurance of death.[12]

So we can see the kenosis of the Father in the events of the cross. But we can also see the Father's kenosis in the post-ascension exaltation of the Son. I mean several things by this statement. As I speculated in *Trinity After Pentecost*, the analogy of the parent stooping to lift a child may not be entirely inappropriate.[13] But even if this analogy fails, it can be acknowledged that the Father divested himself of the right to sole glory in lifting the Son to such

---

10 That the referent of 'finger' and 'power' is the Spirit is contested by Robert P. Menzies (in, e.g., *Empowered for Witness: The Spirit in Luke-Acts* [Sheffield: Sheffield Academic Press, 1994]), but this position has been successfully countered by Max Turner (e.g., in *Power from on High: The Spirit in Israel's Restoration and Witness in Luke-Acts* [Sheffield: Sheffield Academic Press, 1996]).

11 Moltmann, *Crucified God*.
12 Moltmann, *Trinity and Kingdom*, 80.
13 Atkinson, *Trinity After Pentecost*, 132.

heights, to the right hand of his throne (e.g., Acts 2:33). The Father, it seems from early Christian practice, accepted the Son as 'another' divine recipient of believing Christian prayer and worship.[14]

While I write in temporal terms about an event 2,000 years old, these dynamics can be traced into eternity: the eternal generation of the Son was and is the Father's eternal divine choice to empty himself of 'sole rights' to divine glory. In his foreknowledge of the events of the cross, furthermore, the Father's eternal generation of the Son was and is also kenotic. Hans Urs von Balthasar has put this forcibly:

> We shall never know how to express the abyss-like depths of the Father's self-giving, that the Father who, in an eternal 'super-Kenosis,' makes himself 'destitute' of all that he is and can be so as to bring forth a consubstantial divinity, the Son. Everything that can be thought and imagined where God is concerned is, in advance, included and transcended in this self-destitution which constitutes the person of the Father.[15]

We can press this point further. Just as, starting with the events of Pentecost, I found a dynamic reciprocation of kenosis and exaltation unfurling for view, so too in this relationship between the Father and the Son a dynamic reciprocation can be traced. In the eternal generation of the Son, the Father's necessary kenosis leads inexorably to the exaltation of the Son. This is seen in immanent terms, in that the eternally generated Son is divine—the ultimate exaltation.

It is also seen in economic terms, in that in due time the Son's incarnation and crucifixion, which involved the kenosis of the Father as well as the Son, led to the exaltation of the Son in human eyes, following the resurrection and sending of the Spirit. Jesus was in time recognised as divine by those who looked at him with eyes of faith. In turn, too, the kenotic and thereafter exalted Son exalts the Father, both in his spoken praise of the Father during his earthly ministry, and in the eschatological exaltation of the Father that the NT promises (e.g., 1 Cor. 15:28).

It will be noted that I have not sought to decipher a sense in which the Father undergoes kenosis with respect to the Spirit. If this idea does emerge in the economy, I have yet to see it. In terms of God's eternal being, I see a faint hint in the biblical statement that 'God is spirit' (Jn. 4:24). One might also be justified in speculating a kenosis of the Father in his eternal 'spiration' of the Spirit, by way of analogy with the Father's kenosis in generating the Son.

From Irenaeus onwards, great Christian teachers have with good reason referred to the Son and the Spirit as the right and left hands of the Father. Thus analogies can surely be drawn between the two. For example, if it cost the Father, in Balthasar's words, to 'bring forth a consubstantial divinity, the Son', then surely it cost the Father something of his self in bringing forth a consubstantial divinity, the Spirit.

The Father's exaltation of the Spirit

---

[14] For the early history of the development of devotion to Christ as to God, see Larry W. Hurtado, *Lord Jesus Christ* (Grand Rapids, MI; Cambridge: Eerdmans, 2003).

[15] Hans Urs von Balthasar, *Mysterium Paschale* (English Translation; San Francisco: Ignatius Press, 2000 [1970]), viii.

can also be seen by way of analogy with the Son. If, in operating his right hand, the Son, the Father also thereby exalts the Son, so too when the Father operates his left hand, the Spirit, he thereby exalts the Spirit. In all of this, I stress, such exaltation could not occur without the Father's kenosis of himself. It requires the Father's kenosis for there to be an eternal Trinity. It requires the Father's kenosis for the Trinity to act towards humanity, and by extension towards the whole created order.

For all that I have been stressing the Father's kenosis in recent paragraphs, I do not wish to do this to the detriment of affirming the Father's exaltation. This can be seen primally: the generated Son and the spirated Spirit are eternally dependent on the Father for their existence. It can be seen in the economy. The Son and the Spirit are sent into this world by the Father. There is no warrant from scripture for speaking of the Son or the Spirit sending the Father. With particular reference to the Son, in his earthly ministry, the Son obeyed the Father (e.g., Heb. 5:7-9), the Son needed the Father (e.g., Jn. 5:19), and so forth. And it can be seen in the eschaton, when the Father will be 'all in all' (1 Cor. 15:28, where 'God' is clearly the Father). To use the terminology of this article's title, the Father is the 'leader' in the Trinity.

III Equality in the Trinity

By now, my article may have sown confusion about whether I regard the persons of the Trinity as equal. I do, on the simple basis of Christian theism that there is no such thing as semi-divinity or quasi-divinity. Each person of the Trinity is divine and is therefore fully divine. No person is less divine than another, and therefore no person is less than another. But I do not see this equality as a static 'flat' equality. I see it as a dynamic interplay of kenosis and exaltation. Each person humbly lowers self in order to raise the other. Each person, in consequence of such self-abasement, is actually exalted as a result.

A key difficulty that defending equality within the Trinity runs into is its apparent contradiction with the picture presented during Christ's earthly ministry of an incarnate Son who in many ways was subject to the Father (and, arguably, to the leading of the Spirit). This contradiction has been handled in various ways. One way is to regard the persons of the Trinity as equal ontologically but unequal functionally.[16] This apparent explanation of trinitarian relations will not do, for it prises ontology and function unrealistically far apart. In the world of the human, what we are greatly affects what we do; what we do in turn plays a large part in shaping the people we are—so too, presumably, in the world of the divine.

Another apparent explanation would be an appeal to some significant distinction between the immanent Trinity and the economic Trinity (see above for introductory explanation of these terms). In the economy, the Trinity by this argument displays inequality. But the eternal immanent Trinity (surely the real Trinity?) is equal. The weakness of this explanation is obvious: if the immanent Trinity is actually quite

---

16 This is, in effect, the position espoused by Smail in *Like Father, Like Son*, 76.

different from the economic Trinity, then we have no way of knowing anything at all about the immanent Trinity, and the task of trinitarian theology is over.

A third method for explaining the discrepancy between the subordination of Jesus to his Father God and belief in an eternal co-equal Trinity would be to posit that the subordination was displayed only by Christ's human nature, while his divine nature had a quite different relationship to the Father. Again, this apparent explanation is fallacious. Jesus, according to traditional incarnational christology, was one person. The divine nature and human nature did not operate as two independent entities.

Yet another attempt to overcome the problem is to suggest that Jesus submitted to his heavenly Father only temporarily: his resurrection and ascension 'rescued' him from this subordination, which is thus now over.[17] This is clearly no good, for the incarnation of the eternal Word is surely an *accurate*, not a *misleading*, revelation of that Word's eternal relationship with the Father.

By far the most nuanced and well developed explanation of the difficulty is offered by Moltmann and followed by Volf.[18] Yes, they concede: in terms of how, eternally, God 'comes to be' Trinity, one may acknowledge that the Father is the primary cause of the other two. There would be no Son or Spirit without the Father. However, they stress that this 'order of processions' must not be confused with the, so to speak, logically subsequent, relations that result between these three divine persons. In these relations—how each person relates to the others—each is equal.

However, as carefully developed as this idea may be, it still suffers from some of the weaknesses of others surveyed above. To distinguish between the Trinity's processions and the Trinity's relations in the way that Moltmann and Volf do seems as artificial and unhelpful as the distinctions that are sometimes drawn between the economic and the immanent Trinity. All our theologising has to gaze at eternity by means of the limited analogies offered to us time-bound mortals through notions conceived from the passage of time.

Moltmann's and Volf's version uses this analogy to place the processions prior to the ongoing relations, as if somehow the processions are past. God now exists—as Trinity—and each person can get on with relating to the others now that the processions are 'over'. It would be better, I suggest, to think of the processions, too, as ongoing. Using the analogy of the passage of time, it is not so much that the Son is now generated and the Spirit now spirated by the Father and those processions are somehow completed. It is better to think of these processions as eternally ongoing. The Son for all eternity owes his divine eternal life to the Father; so too with the Spirit. The Father eternally upholds their divine existence. Naturally, then, it would be

---

[17] So Kevin Giles, *The Trinity and Subordinationism: The Doctrine of God and the Contemporary Gender Debate* (Downers Grove, IL: InterVarsity Press, 2002).

[18] Moltmann, *Trinity and Kingdom*, 165, 176, 177, 183; Miroslav Volf, *After Our Likeness: The Church as the Image of the Trinity* (Grand Rapids, MI: Eerdmans, 1998), 215-7.

artificial to divide this processional relationship from other aspects of interpersonal relations in the Trinity. The Son relates to the Father as eternally dependent. So too does the Spirit.

At the heart of all these apparent explanations is a failure in their initial assumption. This is that 'equality' is something flat and static, such that equality on the one hand, and kenosis involving submission and so forth on the other hand, are mutually exclusive. Only a being that is unequal need submit. A being that is submitted to is superior.

I see a different picture: the Father is the eternally primary cause of the Trinity relationally as well as 'processionally'. To use other language, relevant to this article, the Father is the leader of the trinitarian persons. However, the equality which the Father shares with the Son and the Spirit is maintained by the Father's eternally kenotic relations with them. The Father is ever emptying his own self into and for the exaltation of the others. The Father is a servant-leader.

IV Applying this Trinitarianism

The concept of servant-leadership is familiar in Christian circles and needs little introduction. In recent decades, popular and semi-popular books on Christian leadership have made it a habit to include sections on the subject. Examples include: C. Peter Wagner's *Leading Your Church to Growth*;[19] Philip King's *Leadership Explosion*;[20] Bob Gordon's *Master Builders*;[21] Tom Marshall's *Understanding Leadership*;[22] David Spriggs' *Christian Leadership*;[23] and Hans Finzel's *The Top Ten Mistakes that Leaders Make*.[24] It is immediately apparent from these works that the term 'servant' in this context indicates not so much that servant-leaders are to be servants of God (true as that is, in Christian eyes). Rather, servant-leaders are to be ones who serve those they lead.

This idea has firm gospel support, to which the books listed above repeatedly refer. This support is to be found both in the example of Jesus and in his commands. While the cross itself is the greatest length to which Jesus' example goes in this regard, perhaps the most famous focused act of example is Jesus' washing of his disciples' feet. It is noteworthy that in his attendant comments, the Johannine Jesus does not disparage leadership. He refers to his own leadership and affirms it: 'You call me "Teacher" and "Lord," and rightly so, for that is what I am' (Jn. 13:13, NIV). It would, admittedly, be reading too much into his next words to imagine that he was calling his disciples to be one another's teachers and lords.

---

[19] Bromley: MARC Europe, 1984. Chapter 3 has sections entitled 'Being Both a Servant and a Leader' and 'Servanthood and Leadership Today'.

[20] Sevenoaks: Hodder and Stoughton, 1987. Chapter 9 is entitled 'Servant Leadership'.

[21] Tonbridge: Sovereign World, 1990. Chapter 7 is entitled 'Called to Serve'.

[22] Chichester: Sovereign World, 1991. Chapter 8 is entitled 'How to Become a Servant Leader'.

[23] Swindon: British and Foreign Bible Society, 1993. Chapter 2 ('What Makes Leadership Christian?') has a section entitled 'The Servant'.

[24] Wheaton, IL: Victor Books, 1994. Chapter 1 is entitled 'The Top-down Attitude'.

Nevertheless, for anyone aspiring to leadership there is a clear call to servanthood: 'Now that I, your Lord and Teacher, have washed your feet, you also should wash one another's feet' (Jn. 13:14, NIV). The same message rings out of the synoptic gospels. In Mark 10, Jesus does not say, 'Whoever wants to become great among you, DON'T!' He says, 'Whoever wants to become great among you must be your servant' (Mk. 10:43, NIV). I do not claim that 'becoming great' is the same as 'becoming a leader', but again it must be clear to the conscientious reader that any form of Christian leadership should involve serving those who are thus led.

Towards the end of the previous section, I introduced Moltmann's and Volf's way of arguing for relational equality in the Trinity. To repeat, while the Father is admittedly the sole cause of the Trinity, the processions of the persons are now logically 'over' and the relations enjoyed between the persons are free from the 'superiority' that the Father had from being the cause of those processions (I use grammatical tenses to convey eternal matters, and acknowledge the huge approximations that result). They are therefore uncomplicatedly equal, through an entire reciprocation within the various intratrinitarian relations. To quote Volf, there are 'symmetrical relations within the Trinity'.[25]

From their view of trinitarian equality come important consequences for leadership in the human realm. Moltmann refers to leadership both in society and in the church.[26] Volf restricts his discussion to ecclesial leadership.[27] Their argument is this: as the church—and so also sometimes wider society—believes God to be and behave, this it reproduces in its own being and behaving. The church has too often seen the Trinity as a hierarchy in which the Father is the eternal autocrat. This belief has led to autocratic, abusive rule of the many by the one in the church and in ecclesially influenced societies.

Understandably, both authors criticise this view of leadership. However, neither author denies the usefulness of leadership altogether. Moltmann concedes, concerning ecclesial leadership, that the 'presbyterial and synodal church order and the leadership based on brotherly advice are the forms of organization that best correspond to the doctrine of the social Trinity'.[28] However, his repeatedly insistent vision is for a 'fellowship of men and women without privilege and subjection'.[29] This is fair enough, but when he presses this further and envisages a situation in which 'authority and obedience are replaced by dialogue, consensus and harmony',[30] he does not reflect the church at its best in the NT, in which dialogue, consensus and harmony seemed to be able to live side-by-side with authority and obedience—with active directing leadership.

Volf too acknowledges a place for leadership, or what he calls ordained office. However, he too is unwilling to

---

25 Volf, *After Our Likeness*, 236.
26 Moltmann, *Trinity and Kingdom*, 192-202.
27 Volf, *After Our Likeness*, ch. VI.
28 Moltmann, *Trinity and Kingdom*, 202.
29 Moltmann, *Trinity and Kingdom*, 165; cf. xiii, 192, 198.
30 Moltmann, *Trinity and Kingdom*, 202.

grant significant leading to officers. Thus for example *'ordination is an act of the entire church led by the Spirit of God, and not simply of one stratum within the church perpetuating itself'*.[31] Again, there is much sentiment here with which I wish to agree. But like Moltmann, Volf goes too far in what he negates, for in denying the possibility of leaders taking the lead in the vital matter of choosing further leaders, Volf so to speak cuts off the life-blood of ongoing leadership.

Both authors write eloquently of the harm hierarchy can do, but both try to swing the pendulum too far the other way, enervating and etiolating leadership while not denying it altogether. And both do this with theological appeal to what, as I have noted, Volf calls a 'symmetrical understanding of the relations between the trinitarian persons'.[32] In fact, Volf's use of the term 'symmetrical' flows over into his ecclesiology: 'the more a church is characterized by symmetrical and decentralized distribution of power and freely affirmed interaction, the more it will correspond to the trinitarian communion.'[33]

It seems to me that the answer to the problem that Moltmann and Volf identify is not so much to posit a relationally 'flat', symmetrically egalitarian Trinity, but to posit one in which there is an eternally, relationally leading Father—but a Father who does so kenotically. Yes, the Father is exalted as leader. But this exaltation is dynamically 'balanced' by real kenosis. To use other language, the leading Father is also—or, rather, thereby—a servant.

To apply my thoughts so far to leadership in today's church and society, I can say that leadership is not a 'dirty word'. It is found eternally in the Trinity. Of course, fallen humanity has developed, consciously and unconsciously, all sorts of leadership patterns that have been abusive of those being led. But if the nature of relationships between humans, especially those in Christ, is in any way to enjoy the overflow of divine life and its patterns seen in the Trinity, in answer to Jesus' high-priestly prayer, this will not most helpfully occur through jettisoning leadership and replacing it with leaderless egalitarianism. It will more helpfully occur by seeking a pattern of leadership that enjoys the overflow of divine love seen in the reciprocal dynamic of kenosis and exaltation in and beyond Pentecost.

Thereby, it will also reflect some of the qualities of human relationship for which the NT calls. The gospel accounts, as I have shown, do not suggest that leadership was abhorred by Jesus. But Jesus referred to his own servanthood as a pattern for the leadership of others. Whether we see this pattern of servant-leadership lived out successfully by the first-generation church that produced the NT documents is debatable. Nevertheless, Jesus' high ideal is clear.

My suggestions about the nature of the eternal trinitarian relations lead me to speculate that when Jesus called his followers, if they aspired to leadership, to aspire to servant-leadership, he was not only seeking to apply wise teaching (in, e.g., 1 Kgs. 12:7) to his follow-

---

31 Volf, *After Our Likeness*, 249, italics original; cf. 2.
32 Volf, *After Our Likeness*, 247; cf. 217, 236.
33 Volf, *After Our Likeness*, 236.

ers' lives, but he was also extending to them by way of instruction the pattern he saw in his own heavenly Father's leadership of him. As he sensed the leadership of the Father in his own life to be that of a servant-leader, so too he sought to live out his own servant-leadership of his disciples and then call them to exercise servant-leadership in their relations with each other.

V The Impact of Servant-Leadership

I close this article by considering the impact of servant-leadership. As the Father's kenotic 'leadership' of the Trinity thereby exalts the Son and the Spirit, so too we can expect that the sort of servant-leadership that answers Jesus' high-priestly prayer will lift those who are being led. With one's faith guided by that prayer, one may trust that servant-leadership patterned after the kenotic relation of the Father with the Son and Spirit will have something of the same effects on those led as the Father has on the Son and Spirit.

Jesus' prayer was for a love between people that mirrored in some way the love between Father and Son. So one can surely expect to find a situation in which servant-leadership does not restrict those who are led but rather lifts them further towards the fulfilment of their potential—it 'exalts' them further towards their being all that they can be.

Furthermore, I suggested earlier that without the kenosis of the Father, there would be no Trinity and there would be no economy. The servant-leadership of the Father, in other words, has led to the successful outworking of divine purposes: the kenosis of the Father serves the activities of the Trinity. This 'teamwork' of the Trinity is not destructive of God's activities but enhancing of them. The long-held metaphor of the Son and the Spirit as the two hands of the Father speaks of harmony and coordination in all divine work.

So in the human sphere, when teams and groups are open to having Jesus' high-priestly prayer answered, at least in part, among them, they will see that servant-leadership does not detract from but rather enhances the outworking of that group's or team's purposes. In all this, truly Christian servant-leadership glorifies God and furthers humanity's redemption.

Vestigia Trinitatis in the Writings of John Amos Comenius and Clive Staples Lewis

Pavel Hošek

Keywords: Enlightenment, Liberalism, sin, apologetics, Augustine, Neo-platonism, revelation, natural theology, education

In this article I would like to point out several interesting parallels in the theological writings of two great Christian thinkers, divided by three centuries and hundreds of miles of distance. The first is the famous British scholar and apologist, C. S. Lewis (1898 - 1963), the second is the last bishop of the Unity of Brethren (a church founded by the radical and pacifist followers of John Huss in Bohemia) and the famous founder of modern educational science, John Amos Comenius (1592 - 1670).

Their cultural and historical contexts were obviously very different. Comenius was a witness of the tragic Thirty Years War (1618 - 1648) which broke out when he was in his middle twenties and which eventually made him (as a committed Protestant) a life-long exile and a homeless reformer of educational systems in several European countries. Lewis lived through both world wars and the cultural and political complexities of the twentieth century. Just as Comenius was a witness of the dramatic religious division of Europe following the sixteenth century Reformation culminating in the Thirty Years War, Lewis was a witness of the serious decline of European Christianity (of all creeds and confessions) due to the secularizing processes initiated by the Enlightenment.

I Facing Enlightenment Reductionist Rationalism

In spite of many important differences between these two faithful Christian scholars, we also find a number of striking similarities. When we compare carefully the main works of these two outstanding Protestant writers, there seems to emerge a similar general framework of their theological thought, as will be shown below. Moreover, in spite of all the historical and cultural differences, their intellectual and religious contexts were similar in one important aspect: both Comenius in the seventeenth century and Lewis in the twentieth century were facing

---

Pavel Hošek, ThD (Charles University), teaches religious studies and ethics at the Evangelical Theological Seminary in Prague and at the Protestant Theological Faculty of Charles University, Prague, Czech Republic. He specializes in relations between Christian theology and religious studies

and fighting what we may call reductionist Enlightenment rationalism.

Comenius had to face its beginning stage, as it was articulated in the writings of early Enlightenment thinkers such as Rene Descartes[1] and especially in the numerous writings and theological claims of the anti-trinitarian Socinians, with whom Comenius intensively debated and polemicized.[2] Lewis had to face and fight a similar sort of reductionist Enlightenment rationalism in its advanced stage, as it was promoted in the writings of liberal Protestant theologians of the nineteenth century and their followers in the twentieth century.[3]

Both Comenius and Lewis were defending orthodox trinitarian theology, based on a high view of Scripture along with a strong emphasis on the orthodox Christology of the early Christian creeds. The challenge of Enlightenment rationalism, in most cases (sooner or later) questioning the trinitarian understanding of God and the related doctrine of Christ's divinity, was perceived not only by Comenius and Lewis, but by many other Christians of their time.

A very common response to that challenge, especially among conservative Protestant theologians, consisted of pointing out the vast difference between the unregenerated and the regenerated mind, i.e. emphasizing the devastating consequences of the Fall in the area of human reason and capacity to know the truth (about God).

In this sense, the challenge of Enlightenment reductionist rationalism was often neutralized by a 'hamartiological' argument: a sinful (godless) mind cannot understand God's truth. As Tertullian claimed, the revealed mystery of God's truth must appear strange and unacceptable, even absurd to natural (unregenerated) man and his earthly wisdom. The problem with this sort of apologetics is that it often sounds convincing only to those who already are convinced. It does not really engage with the challenge, it just delegitimizes its epistemic foundation.

Neither Comenius in the seventeenth century nor Lewis in the twentieth century was satisfied with this sort of defensive apologetics. They refused the tendency of some their contemporaries to defend orthodox Christianity against reductionist rationalism by means of a retreat to an irrationalist, fideistic position (such as Tertullian's 'credo quia absurdum est'; 'I believe because it is absurd'.). Both Comenius and Lewis were convinced that simply quoting the Bible as God's revealed Word and referring to early Christian creeds without any serious interaction with the intellectual challenges of their time was not enough.

Both Comenius and Lewis were profoundly *universalist* thinkers; both of them strongly believed that all truth is God's truth, wherever it is found. Both

---

1 J. Patočka, *Komeniologické studie III* (Praha: Oikumene, 2003), 334ff.
2 J. A. Comenius, *Antisozinianische Schriften*, E. Schadel (ed) (New York, 1983); J. A. Comenius, *Ausgewählte Werke*, vol. IV, part 1-2. Cf. also E. Schadel (ed), *Antisozinianische Schriften* (Deutsche Erstübersetzung), vol I-III (Frankfurt am Main: Peter Lang, 2008). Cf. also the collection of papers in *Studia Comeniana et Historica*, 1989, 11-89.
3 Such as A. T. Robinson's famous *Honest to God* (London: SCM, 1963). Cf. for example C. S. Lewis, 'Fernseed and Elephants', in *Essay Collection* (London: Harper and Collins, 2000), 242ff.

rejected a strict separation between theology and philosophy,[4] between faith and science, between special revelation and general revelation. They were both committed to the principle of the ultimate unity of all truth.[5] In other words, even though both Comenius and Lewis were convinced Protestants, they did not share this type of radical pessimism regarding man's epistemological capacity after the Fall, as it was preached by some of their Protestant contemporaries. Why?

One of the reasons for this (moderate) optimism concerning human epistemic capacity (even *post lapsum*) and also for the interesting similarity in Comenius' and Lewis' general intellectual perspective is the fact that both were strongly influenced by Christian Neo-platonism, as it is found in the writings of Augustine and other great Christian thinkers of this school of thought.[6]

In his time Comenius tried to balance some of the shortcomings of Christian Aristotelianism by developing several key ideas of Christian neo-platonic thinkers, working within the Augustinian tradition of thought,[7] especially the ideas and insights of the great Augustinian neo-platonic thinker Nicolas Cusanus.[8] Lewis was in many respects also a faithful disciple of Augustine,[9] the greatest Christian neo-platonist. He was fascinated also by the Cambridge neo-platonist Henry More[10] (actually Comenius' contemporary).[11] In many respects Lewis' theological position can be adequately described as a version of Christian Neo-platonism.[12]

---

4 Cf. S. Sousedík, 'Komenského filosofie v souvislostech myšlenkového vývoje doby', in *Studia Comeniana et Historica*, 1974, 17f; K. Floss, 'Triády – pojítko mezi filozofií a teologií', in *Studia Comeniana et Historica*, 1994.
5 Concerning Comenius: J. Hábl, *Lessons in Humanity: From the Life and Work of Jan Amos Comenius* (Bonn: VKW, 2011); R. Palouš, *Komenského Boží svět* (Praha: SPN, 1992); J. Patočka, *Komeniologické studie* III, 190ff. Concerning Lewis: A. Barkman, *C. S. Lewis and Philosophy as a Way of Life* (Allentown: Zossima Press, 2009).
6 On the immense influence of Augustine on Comenius see J. Červenka, 'Problematika Komenského metafysiky' in *Studia Comeniana et Historica* III/ 1973; also K. Floss, 'Jan Amos Komenský a trinitární nauka Aurelia Augustina', in *Studia Comeniana et Historica* 2007, 44ff. On Lewis' (neo-)platonism see R. Smith, *Patches of Godlight: The Pattern of Thought of C. S. Lewis* (Athens: Univ. of Georgia Press,

1981); and also A. Barkman, *C. S. Lewis and Philosophy as a Way of Life*, 53ff, 132ff.
7 As K. Floss notes, in Comenius' anti-Socinian writings, Augustine is the most frequently consulted and quoted author. K. Floss, 'Jan Amos Komenský a trinitární nauka Aurelia Augustina', in *Studia Comeniana et Historica*, 2007, 45.
8 P. Floss, 'Komenský a Kusánus', in *Studia Comeniana et Historica*, 1971, 13ff, 20. P. Floss, *Jan Amos Komenský 1670-1970* (Ostrava: Profil, 1970), 71ff.
9 Cf. Barkman, *C. S. Lewis and Philosophy as a Way of Life*, 54f.
10 Barkman, *C. S. Lewis and Philosophy*, 40f.
11 It is worth mentioning that as K. Floss observes, among his contemporaries, Comenius' thinking was closest to the Cambridge neo-platonists. The most influential thinker of this school of thought was H. More, whom Lewis chose as the topic of his dissertation. Cf. K. Floss, 'Angličtí filosofové 17. století a jejich vztah k metafyzice', in *Studia Comeniana et Historica*, 1996, 100.
12 Cf. J. T. Sellars, *Reasoning beyond Reason. Imagination as a Theological Source in the Work of C. S. Lewis* (Eugene: Pickwick Publications, 2011), 4f. and 77ff. Cf. also H. Boersma, *Heavenly Participation* (Grand Rapids: Eerdmans, 2011), 7.

II Reaffirmation of the Trinity

Closely related to this common inspiration in Christian neo-platonic thought is what I consider to be one of the most profound theological similarities between Comenius and Lewis. The key reason for this striking similarity is the fact that both scholars viewed the trinitarian understanding of God as an essential insight not only into the mystery of God's being, but also into the deepest structure of all created reality. This is the reason why they used the trinitarian framework not just as the organizing principle of Christian systematic theology, but actually as an all-inclusive interpretive framework of all reality.

Both Comenius and Lewis—in their general presentation of the Christian view of reality as well as in their apologetic writings against the claims of the anti-trinitarian thinkers among their contemporaries—had the courage to offer a profoundly trinitarian interpretation of all of reality. The Trinity, for both of them, is the most suitable all-inclusive paradigm or organizing principle of all knowledge and indeed of all being. In other words, they both believed that all that exists has a triadic structure, that all reality reflects and mirrors the triadic Divine source of all being.

The very texture of reality is trinitarian. Everything that has been created reflects this triadic structure. Trinity is the noetic and ontological key to all being; it is the key to the enigma of reality, the solution to the puzzle or mystery of all being. Both Comenius and Lewis accepted and developed the Augustinian notion of *vestigia trinitatis*, vestiges of the Trinity, in all creation and in the structure of the human mind. In what follows I will briefly present how Lewis and Comenius elaborated this essential concept into a holistic trinitarian interpretation of reality.

III *Vestigia Trinitatis* in Lewis

For C. S. Lewis, all created reality reflects the Creator: 'Everything God has made has some likeness to Himself.'[13] This implies that (in his understanding) creation also reflects the pattern of intra-trinitarian relations:

> For in self-giving, if anywhere, we touch a rhythm not only of all creation but of all being. For the Eternal Word also gives Himself in sacrifice; and that not only on Calvary. For when He was crucified he did that in the wild weather of His outlying provinces which He had done at home in glory and gladness. From before the foundation of the world He surrenders begotten Deity back to begetting Deity in obedience.[14]

This ineffable relationship between the Father and the Son is actually a third moment or element in itself:

> The union between the Father and Son is such a live concrete thing that this union itself is also a Person... What grows out of the joint life of the Father and Son is a real Person, is in fact the Third of the three Persons who are God.[15]

In this sense Lewis calls the inner life of God 'a dynamic, pulsating activity, a life, almost a kind of drama...

---

13 C. S. Lewis, *Mere Christianity* (New York: Macmillan, 1981), 135.
14 C. S. Lewis, *Problem of Pain* (New York: Macmillan, 1962), 152.
15 Lewis, *Mere Christianity*, 149f.

almost a kind of dance'.[16] This dance consists of the Son's obedient self-surrender to the Father and the Father's generous self-giving to the Son:

> He who from all eternity has been incessantly plunging Himself in the blessed death of self-surrender to the Father can also most fully descend into the horrible and (for us) involuntary death of the body. Because Vicariousness is the very idiom of the reality He has created.[17]

In Lewis' understanding, this 'idiom of reality' is imprinted on all nature. In fact, nature is a 'commentary' on this intratrinitarian relational pattern.[18] It is expressed in the vegetative rhythms of nature, in the periodical death of all life in winter time and the resurrection of all vegetation in spring time:

> In this descent and re-ascent everyone will recognise a familiar pattern: a thing written all over the world. It is the pattern of all vegetable life... It is the pattern of all animal generation too. ... So it is also in our moral and emotional life. Death and Re-birth – go down to go up – it is a key principle. ...The pattern is there in Nature because it was first there in God.[19]

It is also reflected in the mythological stories of pagan religions inspired by vegetative rhythms of nature: 'For the Corn-King is derived (through human imagination) from the facts of Nature, and the facts of Nature from her Creator; the Death and Re-birth pattern is in her because it was first in Him.'[20]

This inner dynamics of intra-trinitarian relations is the deepest foundation of all life (and the most profound definition of what 'life' actually is)[21] and it is also the transcendent prototype and source of all love and the most profound definition of what 'love' means:

> ...the great master Himself leads the revelry, giving Himself eternally to His creatures in the generation, and back to Himself in the sacrifice, of the Word, then indeed the eternal dance makes heaven drowsy with the harmony. All pains and pleasures we have known on earth are early initiations in the movements of that dance... As we draw nearer to its uncreated rhythm... It is Love Himself, and Good Himself.[22]

All human beings (and in a sense all other creatures too) are called to enter into this intra-trinitarian Life and Love and to find their eternal destiny within this intra-trinitarian 'Great dance'.[23] The eschatological destiny of all creation is therefore to enter into the blessed and harmonious inner life of the Trinity.

The practical application of this trinitarian perspective is Lewis' under-

---

16 Lewis, *Mere Christianity*, 149.
17 C. S. Lewis, *Miracles* (London: Geofrey Bles, 1947), 157. For more about Lewis' kenotic understanding of intratrinitarian relations see S. Connoly, *Inklings of Heaven: C. S. Lewis and Eschatology* (Leominster: Gracewing, 2007), 65-75.
18 Lewis, *Miracles*, 157.
19 Lewis, *Miracles*, 135f.

20 Lewis, *Miracles*, 140.
21 Lewis, *Mere Christianity*, 136.
22 Lewis, *Problem of Pain*, 153, cf. also *Mere Christianity*, 149.
23 Lewis, *Mere Christianity*, 138, cf. *Perelandra* (New York: Macmillan, 1947), chapter 17.

standing of Christian life on this earth as gradually entering into this trinitarian pattern of self-surrender or self-giving, of finding one's life by giving it up, which, as Lewis says, is actually practising the steps of the trinitarian 'Great dance' in everyday situations:

> The whole dance, or drama, or pattern of this three-Personal life is to be played out in each one of us ...each one of us has got to enter that pattern, take his place in that dance.[24]

This is how Lewis understands the *imitatio Christi*: Christians, as they relate to God and to fellow human beings, are actually entering Christ's role in the intra-trinitarian relational pattern.

The eschatological goal and 'home' of all humanity (and together with humanity, of all creation) is a blessed participation in the trinitarian life, i.e. entering fully and forever into the Trinity by being drawn into Christ, the second person of the Trinity, by the Holy Spirit, the third person of the Trinity.[25]

IV *Vestigia Trinitatis* in Comenius

J. A. Comenius understands the trinitarian structure of all reality (and the consequent *vestigia Trinitatis*) in a similar, yet also different manner.[26] Like Lewis, he believes that when we carefully observe nature and its order, we can perceive an underlying triadic or trinitarian pattern imprinted in its inner structure. He says in his outline of pansophia:

> What is particular and unique about our method is that all common divisions are triple ... I rejoiced when I understood this harmony of holy trinity, and the more eagerly did I observe it in all other things. ... May therefore this Christian pansophia, opening triple mystery, be consecrated to the eternal triune Lord, powerful, wise, good and forever blessed God.[27]

As we can see from these words, Comenius believes that the archetype of all order and of the structure of all reality is the inner structure of the holy Trinity.[28] He is also convinced that number three is actually primordial; it is 'the first real number'.[29]

---

24 Lewis, *Mere Christianity*, 150.
25 Cf. P. Fiddes, 'On theology', in M. Ward and R. MacSwain, editors, *The Cambridge Companion to C. S. Lewis* (Cambridge University Press, 2010), 89ff.
26 K. Floss observes that Comenius was committed to Augustine's program of tracing *vestigia Trinitatis* in all reality. Cf. *Hledání duše zítřka* (Brno: CDK, 2012), 131.

27 J. A. Comenius *Předchůdce Vševědy*, in *Vybrané spisy (Selected works of) Jan Amos Komenský* 5 (Praha: SPN, 1968), 293 (translation PH). Cf. E. Schadel, 'J. A Comenius Sapientiae trigonus – ein Modell universaler Selbstverwirklichung', in *Studia Comeniana et Historica*, 1986, 29ff; E. Schadel, 'Komenskýs Pansophie als harmonische Einheit von Welt-, Selbst- und Gottes-Erkenntnis', *Studia Comeniana et Historica*, 2008, 24ff.; P. Floss, 'Význam studia patristiky pro pochopení kořenů a povah Komenského díla', in *Studia Comeniana et Historica*, 2007, 11; P. Floss, *Jan Amos Komenský 1670-1970*, 23ff.
28 J. A. Comenius, *De Christianorum Uno Deo, Patre, Filio, Spiritu Sancto* (Amsterodami, 1659), Aph. XXV (AS 55).
29 J. A. Comenius, *Antisozinianische Schriften von Johan Amos Comenius*, edited with introduction by E. Schadel (Hildesheim: Olms, 1983), 51f.

In all his textbooks, educational materials and encyclopaedias, Comenius employs a triadic organizing principle.[30] He believes that it is possible to identify elementary triplets or triads as the most basic categories in all areas of reality.[31] He intentionally organizes all knowledge into sets or systems or structures of three elements or factors. For example, when he speaks about the sources of human knowledge, the world, the mind, and the Bible, he says:

> These three lamps may also rightly be called three books of God, three theatres and three mirrors, also the trinity of God's laws or the trinity of all-inclusive books and three resources of wisdom.[32]

Moreover, Comenius believes that when we analyse the inner functioning of the human mind, we can observe, as Augustine suggested, a footprint of the Trinity in the inner structure of the soul. He speaks about the human mind as 'the image of God, consisting of three parts: reason, will and potentiality'.[33] In his *Panegersia* he says,

Before all things it is known that man is the first among visible creatures, because he was created into God's image. He is therefore similar to God and is a living picture of God's great qualities. And who would not know that with God, three outstanding qualities are emphasized? ...The same three things You find in man.[34]

This conviction was very important for Comenius' educational theory and for his proposals in the area of didactics. His innovative suggestions in the area of education are to a large degree based on his understanding of the triadic structure of human mind and on the three essential powers of the soul.[35]

Another important aspect of Comenius' trinitarianism is his triadic understanding of time and the inner dynamics of history.[36] Drawing on the neo-platonic trinitarian thought of Nico-

---

30 See especially his mature work, *Triertium catholicum*, in *Johannis Amos Comenii Opera omnia* vol. XVIII, edited by V. Balík (Praha, 1974) 246f.

31 J. A. Comenius, *Physicae ad lumen divinum reformatae synopsis*, in *Veškeré spisy Jana Amosa Komenského* vol. I., edited by J. Reber and V. Novák (Brno, 1914), 155. Cf. on Comenius' use of triadistic paradigm as an heuristic tool K. Floss, *Hledání duše zítřka*, 147.

32 J. A. Comenius, 'Panaugia', in *Vybrané spisy (Selected works of) Jan Amos Komenský* vol 4, (Praha: SPN, 1966), 138 (translation PH).

33 J. A. Comenius, 'Pansophia', in *Vybrané spisy JAK* 4, 208 (translation PH).

34 J. A. Comenius, 'Panegersia', in *Vybrané spisy JAK* 4, 82 (translation PH). Cf. E. Schadel, 'Komenskýs Pansophie als harmonische Einheit von Welt-, Selbst- und Gottes-Erkenntnis', *Studia Comeniana et Historica* 2008, 29ff. J. Červenka, 'Problematika Komenského metafysiky', in *Studia Comeniana et Historica* III 1973, 58ff, see also K. Floss' article on Comenius' and Augustine's trinitarian doctrine: 'Jan Amos Komenský a trinitární nauka Aurelia Augustina', *Studia Comeniana et Historica* 2007, 44ff.

35 Such as 'ratio, operatio, oratio'; or 'sapere, agere, loqui', etc. cf. J. Červenka, 'Problematika Komenského metafysiky', *Studia Comeniana et Historica* 1973, 58ff.

36 P. Floss, 'Komenský a Kusánus', in *Studia Comeniana et Historica*, 1971, 26f. See especially U. Voigt, 'Das Geschichtsverständnis des Johann Amos Comenius' in *Via Lucis als kreative Syntheseleistung*, (New York: Peter Lang, 1996).

las Cusanus,[37] Comenius applies the trinitarian interpretative framework in the area of the internal structure of historical developments and events. He believes that the flow of history can be understood as a triadic 'dialectics': the playful activity of Divine wisdom in history operates in accordance with a triadic rhythm: all changes that bring novelty in the flow of history consist of three moments, i.e. they occur in accordance with a triadic outline.

Comenius' trinitarian understanding of history also provided the basic framework for his understanding of eschatology.[38] It was actually his particular understanding of eschatology that made him the founder of modern education and the most influential reformer of educational systems in seventeenth century Europe.

In his understanding, the history of humankind moves towards eschatological peace and harmony. This harmony, which reflects the intra-trinitarian relational harmony, has been lost due to the Fall and sin—but that is not the end of the story. Because of the redeeming work of Christ, the lost harmony will be re-established in the eschatological coming of God's kingdom. In Comenius' understanding, an essential aspect of the expected kingdom will be a final overcoming and reconciliation of all opposites and a restoration of universal harmony reflecting the peace and harmony of Heaven.

This hope was the key motivating factor behind Comenius' educational reforms. He believed that a profound transformation of educational systems is needed as a preparation for the coming eschatological climax of human history, the establishing of God's kingdom.

V Conclusion

As we have seen, the respective applications of the all-inclusive trinitarian framework of thought in Comenius and Lewis are quite similar (yet also different). The way they understood *vestigia Trinitatis*, identifiable in all creation and providing an essential and illuminating insight into the inner structure of all reality, betrays a common origin of this perspective in the Christian adaptation of neo-platonic thought, especially as found in the writings of Augustine and his followers, which was their common source of inspiration.

Both Comenius and Lewis and the immense influence of their works, which (in both cases) seems to be growing with time, are an important witness to the illuminating and heuristic potential of trinitarian thought. This is the case not just as a reflection and articulation of the central mystery of Christian faith, but also as an inexhaustible source of inspiration and insight in all serious thinking about the 'depth grammar' and internal structure of all created reality.

---

37 On the influence of Cusanus' trinitarianism and triadism (especially the triad materia, forma, connexio) on Comenius (and his universal triad materia, spiritus, lux) see J. Patočka, *Komeniologické studie* III (chapter 'Triády Cusanovy a triády Komenského') 280ff, see also J. Červenka, 'K problematice vztahů Komenského ke Campanellovi', in *Studia Comeniana et Historica* 1985, 7ff.; see also P. Floss, *Jan Amos Komenský 1670-1970*, 71ff, and J. Červenka, 'Problematika Komenského metafysiky', in *Studia Comeniana et Historica* 1973, 30f, 54.

38 Cf. on Comenius' eschatology J. Hábl, *Lessons in Humanity*, 90ff.

Both Comenius and Lewis were facing and fighting Enlightenment reductionist rationalism with its anti-trinitarian tendencies. Comenius was facing its early manifestations (Socinian thinkers among his contemporaries), Lewis was facing its mature forms (reductionist theologies of liberal Protestantism). In facing the challenge of Enlightenment rationalist anti-trinitarianism, both Comenius and Lewis rejected the anti-intellectual and fideistic response to that challenge as presented by some of their Christian contemporaries. Both proposed instead a courageous universal interpretive framework of all reality, which was unapologetically trinitarian. And as we have seen, both exercised great creativity in developing a holistic 'trinitarian hermeneutics'.

Now the Enlightenment reductionist rationalism in theology is going through a serious crisis and the relativistic or irrationalist postmodern alternatives do not seem to provide any firm epistemological basis for responsible theological thinking. I would therefore suggest that the sort of trinitarian intellectual framework which Comenius and Lewis tried to develop seems to offer a promising and inspiring way forward for Christian theologians faithful to the orthodox teachings of the church and at the same time struggling with the intellectual challenges of the contemporary cultural situation.

'Bones to Philosophy, but milke to faith' – Celebrating the Trinity

Tersur Aben

KEYWORDS: *Creeds, revelation, baptism, salvation, benediction, burial, spiritual lives*

I Trinity and Faith

Theological discussions of the doctrine of Trinity have, in recent years, centred on the relationship between the three divine persons. In those discussions, theologians tend to focus on explicating the threeness/oneness relationship in God. Some theologians start from the oneness of God, which they take as given, and they go on to say how one God is three persons.[1] Other theologians start from the three persons of God, which they take as given, and they go on to say how three distinct persons are one God.[2]

The impression one gets from some discussions is that the Trinity has been reduced to a forum for theologians to explore the logical relationship between the oneness and the threeness of God. Thus, Neal Plantinga says, 'Trinity doctrine in fact bristles with problems and questions. But dwarfing all others in things Trinitarian is the central conceptual problem of threeness and oneness.'[3] One cannot help but feel that some contemporary theologians see the Trinity as a mathematical puzzle or a logical riddle to be solved via clever analogies or thought-experiments.[4]

Failing to see how Trinity applies to Christian life, some may concur with Immanuel Kant who says:

> The doctrine of the Trinity, taken literally, has no practical relevance at

---

[1] Famous theologians in the western Church such as Augustine, Anselm, and Aquinas can be named here. Modern theologians that take this position include Karl Barth, Wolfhart Pannenberg, and Brian Leftow.
[2] Famous theologians in the eastern Church such as Gregory of Nyssa, Gregory of Nazianzus, and Basil can be named here. In modern times we can include such theologians as Jürgen Moltmann, Neal Plantinga, and Richard Swinburn.
[3] Cornelius Plantinga Jr., 'The Threeness/Oneness Problem of the Trinity', *Calvin Theological Journal* (23:1 April 1988): 38.
[4] Plantinga Jr., 'The Threeness/Oneness Problem', 37-53. Brian Leftow, 'Anti Social Trinitarianism', *The Trinity*, ed. Stephen T. Davis, Daniel Kendall and Gerald O'Collins (Oxford: Oxford University Press, 1999), 203-249.

Rev Tersur A Aben is Provost and Professor of Philosophy and Systematic Theology at the Theological College of Northern Nigeria, Bukuru, Jos. He earned his PhD in Systematic Theology from Calvin Theological Seminary, Grand Rapids, MI, USA.

all, even if we think we understand it; and it is even more clearly irrelevant if we realize that it transcends all our concepts. Whether we are to worship three or ten persons in the Deity makes no difference.[5]

Similarly, F. D. E. Schleiermacher says: 'Our faith in Christ and our living fellowship with him would be the same even if we had no knowledge of any such transcendent fact [as the Trinity] and even if the fact itself were different.'[6] Karl Rahner adds that some find the Trinitarian faith irrelevant to the way many Christians live. 'Despite their orthodox confession of the Trinity, Christians are, in their practical life, almost mere monotheists.'[7]

But the biblical teaching that God is Trinity of persons has nothing to do with mathematics or the logic of relations. Rather, the Bible reveals that God is a Trinity in order to spell out how each divine person worked our salvation and to reveal the fullness of God to us. We know God is Trinity because the Bible says so. Our salvation is the gracious indivisible work of three divine persons. We are saved by God the Father through the Son, Jesus Christ, and by the power of the Holy Spirit.[8]

Although the Bible does not use the term Trinity in the way the Lateran church councils used it, early Christians were aware that the Trinity is at the heart of biblical revelation about God. As the church put its faith in Jesus Christ and thanked God for our salvation from sin, it knew that our salvation is from the Father, through the Son, and by the power of the Holy Spirit. Thus, the church affirmed the Trinity and taught Christians to embrace the Trinity.

Not only did the church believe that Jesus Christ spoke truthfully when he said that he and the Father are one and that he is in the Father and the Father is in him, but it taught that in speaking so, Jesus Christ was attesting to a unique relationship of equality between him and the Father. This is why Jesus Christ avers: 'If anyone loves me, he will obey my teaching. My father will love him and *we* will come to him and make *our* home with him' (Jn. 14:23; my italics).

However, Jesus Christ did not limit this relationship to himself and the Father; rather he extends it to the Holy Spirit. Thus, Jesus says: 'But the counsellor, the Holy Spirit, whom the Father will send, in my name, will teach you all things and will remind you of everything I have said to you' (Jn. 23:26). It is evident from these passages that Jesus Christ wanted us to know that God is Father, Son, and Holy Spirit.

Instead of showing how the Trinity applies to our Christian lives, theologians have dwelt on the relationship that

---

5 Immanuel Kant, *Religion and Rational Theology*, trans. A. W. Wood and G. di Giovanni, The Cambridge Edition of the Works of Immanuel Kant (Cambridge: Cambridge University Press, 1996), 264.
6 Friedrich D. E. Schleiermacher, *The Christian Faith*, trans. H. R. Mackintosh and J. S. Stewart (Edinburgh: T & T Clark, 1928), 741.
7 Karl Rahner, *The Trinity*, trans. J. Donceel (New York: Crossroad Pub., 1977), 10.
8 Cf. Philip W. Butin, *Revelation, Redemption, and Response: Calvin's Trinitarian Understanding*

of the Divine-Human Relationship (New York: Oxford University Press, 1995), 26-94; Gerald Bray, *The Doctrine of God* (Downers Grove, Ill.: Inter-Varsity Press, 1993), 197-212.

holds between the three divine persons and the implication of Trinity on the oneness of God. The church developed the language of Trinity to account for biblical references to plurality in God. While that language of Trinity effectively explains Old Testament references to God in the plural (such as Gen. 1:26; 3:22; 11:7; Is. 6:8) it failed to adequately apply the Trinity to our Christian lives.

The language of Trinity effectively explains the mysterious trio that visited Abraham at Mamre (Gen. 18:1-22) and other references to three, such as angelic appearances and the three disciples who formed the inner circle of Jesus. But clearly, these references fell short of stating hypostatic distinction in God, which grounds the doctrine of Trinity. It is at the baptism of Jesus Christ that we clearly *see* that God is a Trinity of persons. So we shall start our discussion of the Trinity from the baptism of Jesus Christ.

II Trinity and Baptism

At the baptism of Jesus Christ we encounter the ultimate reality that God is Trinity. We hear the Father testifying about Jesus Christ, saying: 'This is my Son whom I love; with him I am well pleased' (Mt. 3:17) and we see the Holy Spirit descend like a dove on Jesus Christ at baptism. These events convinced John the Baptist that Jesus is the Christ (the Messiah) of whom he proclaimed that one greater than himself was coming to take away the sins of the world.

The testimony of the Father about Jesus Christ and the descent of the Holy Spirit on Jesus Christ reveal the true identity of God as Trinity of co-equal persons who work together to save us from sin. The convergence of the Trinitarian persons at the baptism of Jesus Christ makes us know without a doubt that God is Trinity.

Our baptism recalls the convergence on the Trinity, so Jesus instructs his disciples on how they should baptize believers saying:

> All authority in heaven and on earth has been given to me. Go therefore and make disciples of all nations, baptizing them in the name of the Father and of the Son and of the Holy Spirit, and teaching them to obey everything that I have commanded you (Mt. 28:18-20).

Baptism links us in a unique way to the Father, the Son, and the Holy Spirit. Baptism symbolizes that our salvation is through the Trinity. Thus, Peter describes the baptized as: [Those] 'who have been chosen and destined by God the Father and sanctified by the Holy Spirit to be obedient to Jesus Christ and to be sprinkled with his blood' (1 Pet. 1:2).

Similarly, Philip W. Butin says that baptism convinces us that the Father, the Son, and the Holy Spirit are one God. Only after the church sealed its faith in Trinity would it make sense for theologians to explain how three distinct divine persons are one God:

> This is where the path toward the full recognition of God's Tri-unity begins. In the New Testament and the early church, baptized followers of Jesus struggled for adequate terminology to express their growing awareness that Father, Son, and Holy Spirit are each genuinely divine and also intimately united with one another, both in God's own

divine reality and in God's work in human lives and in the world.⁹

Baptism brings believers into perfect fellowship with the three divine persons and makes them participate in the life, ministry, suffering, death, resurrection, ascension and enthronement of the Son in heaven.

No wonder then that Jürgen Moltmann characterizes baptism as the event that puts us into the life of the Trinity and makes us stop thinking of the Trinity as a mathematical or logical problem to be solved by smart theologians. The Trinity becomes real to us in baptism and baptism makes us participants in the history of the Trinitarian persons.¹⁰ By participating in the life of the Father, Son, and Holy Spirit we gain a new identity as God's children and co-heirs with the Son.

III Trinity and Salvation

Our salvation is essentially a Trinitarian affair. It is precisely for the sake of redeeming us from sin that the Father sent the Son to suffer and die on Calvary. Paul attests:

> When the fullness of time had come, God sent his Son, born of a woman, born under the law, in order to redeem those who were under the law, so that we might receive adoption as God's sons and daughters. Because you are his sons and daughters, God sent the spirit of his Son into our hearts, the Spirit who calls out, 'Abba, Father'. So you are no longer slaves, but God's children; and since you are his children, he has made you also heirs' (Gal. 4:4-5).

Through the work of the Holy Spirit God restores us to perfect fellowship with God and we cease to be enemies of God. We are now children of God in Christ and by the power of the Holy Spirit we are the glory of God on earth. By the empowering of the Holy Spirit, Christians all over the world are one before God even though they are many.

Already by c. 190 A.D. Irenaeus taught all believers to confess faith in Trinity in order to be saved:

> The Church, though dispersed throughout the whole world, even to the ends of the earth, has received from the apostles and their disciples this faith: in one God, the Father Almighty, Maker of heaven and earth, and the sea, and all things that are in them; and in one Christ Jesus, the Son of God, who became incarnate for our salvation and in the Holy Spirit.¹¹

But the need for a statement of the church's belief about the Trinity became evident when theologians and churchmen put forth conflicting theories about the identity of God and about the relationship that holds between the three divine persons.

The first set of disputes were about the identity of God, which arose with Marcion who had broken with the church (in the second century) in

---

9 Philip W. Butin, *The Trinity* (Louisville, Kentucky: Geneva Press, 2001), 14.
10 Jürgen Moltmann, *The Trinity and the Kingdom*, trans. Margaret Kohl (San Francisco: Harper and Row, 1981), 95.
11 Cf. Philip W. Butin, *The Trinity* (Louisville, KT.: Geneva Press, 2011), 18. Romans 10:9: 'If you confess that Jesus is Lord and believe in your heart that God raised him from the dead then you will be saved.'

teaching that the Old Testament God was different from the New Testament God. The church rejected Marcionism by affirming the oneness of God who created all things and who sent his Son to save the world from sin. One and the same God revealed himself in the Old Testament and through Jesus Christ in the New Testament.

Another dispute was over the salvation that God gave us through the Son by the power of the Holy Spirit and it was tagged Gnosticism. Gnosticism taught that salvation consists in the enlightenment of the soul or a religious awakening of the soul towards Christ. Gnosticism denied that Jesus Christ was the true saviour of the world or the restorer of our communion with God. Against Gnosticism, the church reiterated its faith in God who is Father, Son, and Holy Spirit. The church affirmed that Jesus Christ alone is the saviour of the world. No level of enlightenment could save humans from sin. Rather, salvation is a free gift of God to humans that costs God the death of his only begotten Son.

Praxeas took the opposite direction by blurring the distinction between the Father, the Son, and the Holy Spirit. Praxeas taught that making personal distinction in God amounts to polytheism or a rejection of God's perfect oneness. To avoid polytheism, therefore, Praxeas denied Trinity. In response to Praxeas, Tertullian observed that there is difference between that in which God is one—*Substance* and that in which God is three—*Person*. Tertullian said that Christians believe in one God who is three distinct divine persons. The three divine persons are distinct, but not separate and this preserves God's oneness.[12]

The other set of disputes were over the relationship between the Father, the Son, and the Holy Spirit. The first disputed view was *subordinationism*, which taught that the Son and the Holy Spirit are below the Father. The second disputed view was *modalism*, which taught that only one divine person exists and he revealed himself to us as Father, Son, and Holy Spirit.[13] Father, Son, and Holy Spirit are names for different modes of the one divine person.

The church rejected subordinationism for ranking the Son and the Holy Spirit below the Father. Also, the church rejected modalism for blurring the distinction between the three divine persons. At the Council of Nicea, 325, the church reiterated its faith in the equality of the Trinitarian persons (contra Arius) by teaching that Father, Son, and Holy Spirit have one divine substance. Thus, Nicea describes Jesus Christ as: 'God from God, Light from Light, true God from true God, begotten, not created, of the same reality as the Father, through him all things were made'.[14]

The church summed up its faith in Trinity saying: 'We believe in one God the Father almighty ... And in one Lord Jesus Christ, the only Son of God ...

---

[12] Tertullian, *On Modesty*, 21; see, A. Roberts and J. Donaldson, eds. *Ante-Nicene Fathers* (Peabody, Mass.: Hendricksen Publishers, 1994), 4:99.

[13] Cornelius Plantinga, Jr., 'Trinity', in *The International Standard Bible Encyclopedia*, General Ed., Geoffrey W. Bromiley (Grand Rapids: William B. Eerdmans Pub. Co., 1988), 914-921.

[14] Nicene Creed (325).

And we believe in the Holy Spirit the Lord, the giver of life'.[15] The Athanasian Creed begins with this preamble:

> Whoever desires to be saved should above all hold to the catholic faith. Anyone who does not keep it whole and unbroken will doubtless perish eternally. Now this is the catholic faith: 'That we worship one God in trinity and the trinity in unity, neither blending their persons nor dividing their essence...'[16]

The Apostles' Creed states its faith in Trinity from a personal point of view. 'I believe in God, the Father almighty ... I believe in Jesus Christ, his only Son, our Lord ... I believe in the Holy Spirit.'[17]

Later, during the Reformation, the church developed texts such as the Heidelberg Catechism in question and answer form to teach the basic tenets of Christianity and to prepare new converts for baptism and communion. In moving word it says, '[We] belong, body and soul, in life and in death, not to [ourselves], but to [our] faithful saviour Jesus Christ', and then it explains the content of what we believe around the three articles of the Apostles' Creed, showing how the entire faith is trinitarian.[18]

The Trinity is thus at the heart of Christian faith and worship of God. We worship God as Father, Son, and Holy Spirit. It is the triune God who saves us and restores us back into fellowship with God. Salvation brings us into perfect and loving fellowship with the Father, through the atoning death of the Son, and by the power of the Holy Spirit. The Father initiated our salvation, the Son saved us by his death on Calvary, and the Holy Spirit applies salvation into our lives.

Perceiving Trinity as the heart of Christian faith in God, Gerald O'Collins says:

> Nowadays the widespread appreciation of the Trinitarian face of the whole story of Jesus—from his virginal conception and baptism right through to the resurrection, the outpouring of the Holy Spirit, and his coming in glory at the end—functions against such a failure to ground Christology in Trinitarian doctrine.[19]

Similarly, Jürgen Moltmann insists that we can understand the words and work of Jesus Christ for our redemption only from the point of view of the Trinity. In the life and death of Jesus Christ, we see and appreciate the full inner-Trinitarian drama that saves us from sin and restores us back into fellowship with God.[20]

Essentially, thinking about the Trinity from the point of view of baptism and salvation links us directly to the Trinity. Thus, the Trinity ceases to be a mere doctrine that generates math-

---

15 *The Nicene Creed* (325A.D.), cited in *Trinity Hymnal* (Swanee, GA: Great Commission Publication Inc., 1990), 846.
16 *The Athanasian Creed*, cited in *Psalter Hymnal* (Grand Rapids: CRC Publications, 1988).
17 Wolfhart Pannenberg, *The Apostles' Creed: in the Light of Today's Questions*, trans. Margaret Kohl (Philadelphia: Westminster Press, 1972).
18 *Heidelberg Catechism* Q. & A. 1.
19 Gerald O'Collins, SJ, 'The Holy Trinity: The State of the Questions', in *The Trinity*, 3.
20 Jurgen Moltmann, *Trinity and the Kingdom*, trans. Margaret Kohl (London: SCM Press, 1981).

ematical problem of numbers or logical problem of relations in God. Instead, the Trinity becomes a potent means by which we express our vibrant faith in God the Father who saves us through the Son and by the power of the Holy Spirit.

IV Trinity and Benediction

In the Scriptures, the fellowship or communion we have with the Trinity was expressed in benediction. Benediction is a short prayer for God to bless believers and for the commune with God to never cease. In the benediction, the Apostle or Pastor asks God to dispense special gifts of grace, love, and peace to believers. Believers are to remain connected with God the Father, through the Son, and by the power of the Holy Spirit. Although believers are different people, they are made one in Christ through the Holy Spirit.

Knowing that God is a Trinity of persons shapes our relationship with God. Thus Jeremy Taylor says that Christian prayer is always to the Trinity:

> God being one in nature, is also three in person; expressed in the Scripture by the names of Father, Son, and Holy Spirit. The first person is known to us by the name of the Father of our Lord Jesus Christ. The second person is called the Son and the Word of the Father. The third is the Spirit and promise of the Father. And these are three and one after a secret manner which we must believe but cannot understand.[21]

For Taylor, prayer always expresses our worship and devotion to the Father, the Son, and the Holy Spirit. Similarly, Lewes Bayly says that we can properly pray to God only if we believe that God is Trinity. 'In sum', Bayly says, 'a proper understanding of the Trinity removes idolatry, focuses prayer, and encourages true devotion and knowledge'.[22]

V Baptism and Burial

The Trinity is the driving force for the faith of the saints who look to the coming age and the end of time. The saints know that this age shall give way to another age in which we shall come before the throne of God to celebrate the victory of the Father, Son, and Holy Spirit over the kingdom of darkness. Looking forward to that celebration with the Trinity, the church buries saints (who die in the Lord) in the name of the Father, the Son, and the Holy Spirit. At the burial of the saint, the minister packs sand but instead of saying dust to dust the minister says the words of baptism: 'I bury you in the name of the Father, the Son, and the Holy Spirit.' All the saints by the graveside reply, 'Amen'. In this way the church completes the circle of Christian walk that began at baptism in the Trinity and ends at burial in the Trinity.

The minister may close the burial ceremony with benediction. For in-

---

21 Jeremy Taylor, 'The Golden Grove', in *The Whole Work of the Right Rev. Jeremy Taylor* (15 vols., London: Moyes, 1928), XV. 12-33.

22 Lewes Bayly, *The Practice of Pietie* (London: 1631), 52; cited in Philip Dixon, *Nice and Hot Disputes: The Doctrine of the Trinity in the Seventeenth Century* (London and New York: T & T Clark, 2003), 9.

stance, the burial form of the Christian Reformed Church ends with this benediction: 'The peace of God, which transcends all understanding, guard your hearts and your minds in Christ Jesus. And may the blessing of almighty God, Father, Son and Holy Spirit, remain with you always. Amen.'[23] Here again we see that the Trinity is not just a doctrine that speaks about numbers in God. Rather, the Trinity defines our Christian life—it makes us a people called into new life with the Father, Son, and Holy Spirit—starting at baptism and ending at death. John Donne (1572-16331) states this view of Trinity best in the Litany of Saints:

> O Blessed glorious Trinity,
> Bones to Philosophy, but milke to faith
> Which are wise serpents, diversely
> Most sliperinesse, yet most entanglings hath
> As you distinguish'd undistinct
> By power, love, knowledge bee,
> Give mee a such selfe different instinct
> Of these let all mee element bee,
> Of power, to love, to know, you unnumbered three.[24]

Donne's remark that the Trinity is to philosophers a difficult doctrine but it is a celebration of life to saints is quite incisive. The grave no longer has power over saints because it is conquered by the Trinity.

The Trinitarian pronouncement at burial calls to mind God's total victory over death. As the writer of Hebrews says:

> God shared in humanity so that by his death he might break the power of him who holds the power of death—that is, the devil—and free those who all their lives were held in slavery by their fear of death (Heb. 2:14).

Saints face death with tranquillity because they know that Christ has vanquished death. Thus, Paul asks: 'O death, where is your sting? O Grave, where is your victory?' (1Cor. 16:55).

Believers in Christ no longer tremble at the thought of death. Death is a means to get to see our Lord face to face. To be present with our Lord in his Father's house where he is preparing a place for us is the greatest expectation of the saints. Thus, Theophane Venard writes:

> I shall be beheaded. Within a few short hours my soul will quit this earth, exile over, and battle won. I shall mount upwards and enter into our true home. There among God's elect I shall gaze upon what eye of man cannot imagine, hear undreampt of harmonies, enjoy a happiness the heart cannot comprehend.[25]

Similarly, Theresa of Avila expressed her longing for union with the Lord in heaven through death saying: 'Bridegroom and Lord, the longed-for hour has come! It is time for us to see

---

[23] *Worship Handbook: Creeds and Liturgical Forms*, eds. Timothy Palmer and Tersur Aben (Jos: ACTS, 2005), 126.

[24] John Donne, *Complete English Poems*, ed. C. A. Patrides (London: Dent, 1994), cited in Philip Dixon, *Nice and Hot Disputes*, 22-23.

[25] Thoephane Venard, *The Wisdom of the Saints: An Anthology*, ed. Jill Haak Adels (Oxford & New York: Oxford University Press, 1987), 196.

one another, my Beloved, my Master. It is time for me to set out. Let us go.'[26]

VI Trinity and the Heart of God

This brief study tries to show how Christians apply the biblical truth that God is Trinity to their lives on earth as they look forward to the perfect, uninterrupted communion with God in heaven. I show that, for many Christians, the Trinity is not a mathematical puzzle or a logical enigma to be solved via clever analogies or thought-experiments. Neither do they try to conceal the reality of Trinity under a thousand qualifications that basically present God as one person in three modes of being.

Rather, the Trinity is the heart of God's self-disclosure to and involvement with humans on earth. The experience of God by Israel from Exodus to Canaan concretizes God as personal. The experience of God from Incarnation to Eschatology concretizes God as three distinct divine persons. The mission of the church is thus to proclaim the gospel of salvation and the restoration of humans back to God, which the Son accomplished on Calvary and the Holy Spirit applied to believers at Pentecost.

---

[26] Theresa of Avila, *The Wisdom of the Saints*, 193.

Appendix
The Trinity in the Bible and Selected Creeds of the Church

Compiled by Thomas K. Johnson

I In the Bible

This study assumes that the classical Christian teaching on the Trinity is consistent with the Bible, though this claim will not be documented at length. The reader who is uncertain that the Triune nature of God is taught in the Bible should carefully consider some of the many relevant biblical texts on this theme. Though the technical language of the classical Christian creeds is not used in the Bible, this careful way of speaking about God flows organically from the entire Bible. A few selected texts which the reader may want to consider:

- Matthew 3:13-17; Mark 1:9-13; Luke 3:21-22; John 1:29-34
- Matthew 28:18-20
- John 1:1-18
- John 14:16, 26; 15:26-27; John 16:5-15
- Romans 1:1-6
- 2 Corinthians 13:14
- Ephesians 1:3-14; 2:14-22
- Colossians 1:15-18
- 1 Peter 1:1-2

Though the teaching about the Trinity comes mostly in the New Testament, there are many places where the Old Testament points toward understanding God as a Trinity. This is sometimes connected with descriptions of complexity within the Godhead, sometimes with clear distinctions between the work of God as Creator and as Redeemer.

Some of these texts are:

- Genesis 1:26-27
- Isaiah 43:10-11; 44:6; 48:16; 63:7-16
- Psalm 2
- Psalm 45:6-7
- Psalm 110

Our understanding of the Trinity is closely associated with our understanding of Jesus, the Christ, who is fully God and fully man, yet one Person. This classical Christian teaching is also assumed in this study, though it will not be defended

at length. A few biblical texts the reader may wish to consider on this topic, in addition to the Psalms mentioned above:
- Isaiah 9:6-7
- Daniel 7:13-14
- Zechariah 12:10
- Matthew 9:1-8; 11:25-30; 14:22-32
- Mark 4:35-41
- John 3:16-36; 5:16-27; 20:24-29
- Romans 5:15-17; 9:1-5
- 1 Corinthians 2:6-10
- Colossians 2:9
- Hebrews 1:1-13; 2:5-18; 4:14-16; 5:7-9
- 1 John 1:1-4; 4:1-3
- 2 John 7-8

II Early Christian Creeds
A. The Creed before the Apostles' Creed

From the early centuries of the church Christians used summaries of the faith to maintain consistency of basic teaching among the churches and from generation to generation. There were a few very similar creeds that were slowly replaced by the 'Apostles' Creed'. As an example of a creed of which we have a complete text that was a forerunner of the Apostles' Creed we include the creed of Irenaeus (130-202 AD).

> Although the church is dispersed throughout the world, even to the ends of the earth, it has received this common faith from the apostles and their disciples:
>
> [We believe] in one God, the Father Almighty, Maker of heaven and earth and the sea, and everything that is in them
>
> And in one Christ Jesus, the Son of God, who became incarnate for our salvation
>
> And in the Holy Spirit, who proclaimed the [divine] dispensations through the prophets, including the advents, the birth from a virgin, the passion, the resurrection from the dead and the bodily ascension into heaven of the beloved Christ Jesus our Lord, as well as his [future] coming from heaven in the glory of the Father, when he will 'gather all things in one'.[1] And to raise up again all flesh of the whole human race, in order that 'every knee should bow and every tongue confess'[2] to Christ Jesus, our Lord and God, our Savior and king, according to the will of the invisible Father, and that he should execute right-

---

1 Eph. 1:10
2 Phil. 2:10-11
3 Eph. 6:12

eous judgment toward all. That he may send 'the spirits of wickedness'[3] and the angels who transgressed and became apostates, together with the ungodly and unrighteous, wicked and profane among human beings, into everlasting fire, but in the exercise of his grace may grant immortality to the righteous and holy, and to those who have kept his commandments and persevered in his love and may clothe them with everlasting glory.[4]

B. The Apostles' Creed

The Apostles' Creed was not written by the apostles but it contains the central elements of the gospel proclaimed by the apostles and is apostolic in that sense. (We have not seen convincing evidence for the claim, repeated occasionally in Christian history, that there was a council of the apostles in the first century which wrote this creed.) With very slight variations in wording, it has been used as a simple summary of central Christian beliefs since very early in Christian history. Almost this exact wording has been used since about 390 AD.

In early Christian history it was recited, especially at the time of baptism, as a Triune statement of faith which nicely explained baptism 'in the name of the Father and of the Son and of the Holy Spirit'. This creed is one of the sources of the common Christian way of talking about 'Three Articles' of the faith, about the Father, about the Son, and about the Holy Spirit. This outline shows how the early church saw the doctrine of the Trinity as not only central to knowing God but also the leading way to outline the entire faith.

I believe in God the Father Almighty, Maker of heaven and earth;
And in Jesus Christ his only Son, our Lord:
Who was conceived by the Holy Spirit,
Born of the Virgin Mary,
Suffered under Pontius Pilate, was crucified, dead, and buried;
He descended into hell;
The third day he arose again from the dead,
He ascended into heaven and sits at the right hand of God the Father Almighty;
From thence he shall come to judge the living and the dead.
I believe in the Holy Spirit,
The Holy Catholic Church, the communion of the saints,
The forgiveness of sins, the resurrection of the body, and the life everlasting.

C. The Nicene Creed

The 'Nicene Creed' contains the teaching approved by the Council of Nicea in 325, but the exact wording and format come from the Council of Constantinople in 381. (In contrast, the exact wording of the creed approved at Nicea is sometimes

---

4 This quotation is taken from Gerald L. Bray, (Ed.), *We Believe in One God* (Intervarsity Press, 2009), 4, quoting Irenaeus, *Prescriptions Against Heretics*.

called 'The Creed of Nicea.') For this reason it is sometimes also called 'The Creed of Constantinople' or 'The Nicene-Constantinopolitan Creed'. The teaching of the creeds from Nicea and Constantinople were fully approved at the Council of Chalcedon in 451. The text of the Nicene Creed follows:

> We believe in one God the Father All-sovereign, maker of heaven and earth, and of all things visible and invisible;
>
> And in one Lord Jesus Christ, the only-begotten Son of God, Begotten of the Father before all the ages, Light of Light, true God of true God, begotten not made, of one substance (homoousion) with the Father, through whom all things were made; who for us men and for our salvation came down from the heavens, and was made flesh of the Holy Spirit and the Virgin Mary, and became man, and was crucified for us under Pontius Pilate, and suffered and was buried, and rose again on the third day according to the Scriptures, and ascended into the heavens, and sits on the right hand of the Father, and comes again with glory to judge the living and the dead, of whose kingdom there shall be no end;
>
> And in the Holy Spirit, the Lord and the Life-giver, that proceeds from the Father,[5] who with the Father and the Son is worshipped together and glorified together, who spoke through the prophets:
>
> In one holy Catholic and Apostolic Church:
>
> We acknowledge one baptism unto remission of sins. We look for a resurrection of the dead, and the life of the age to come.[6]

D. The Definition (or Creed) of Chalcedon

This creed is often called a definition, not a creed, because its focus is on defining the relation between the two natures of Christ, not on confessing our entire trinitarian Christian faith. It is included here because the Christian understanding of the Trinity is closely associated with the Christian understanding of Jesus, the Christ, being both fully God and fully human. It was adopted by the Council of Chalcedon (also called the Fourth Ecumenical Council) in 451 AD. It has been generally accepted by most Christians except those who belong to the Oriental Orthodox Churches.

> We, then, following the holy Fathers, all with one consent, teach people to confess one and the same Son, our Lord Jesus Christ, the same perfect in Godhead and also perfect in manhood;
>
> truly God and truly man, of a reasonable [rational] soul and body;

---

5 At this point the western churches later added the phrase 'and the Son' (*filioque* in Latin) to indicate that the Holy Spirit was sent out at Pentecost by both the Father and the Son and has similar relationships with the Father and the Son.

6 This text is taken from *Documents of the Christian Church,* second edition, selected and edited by Henry Bettenson (Oxford University Press, 1963), 26. (English spelling and grammar modernized).

consubstantial [co-essential] with the Father according to the Godhead, and consubstantial with us according to the Manhood;

in all things like unto us, without sin;

begotten before all ages of the Father according to the Godhead, and in these latter days, for us and for our salvation, born of the Virgin Mary, the Mother of God, according to the Manhood;

one and the same Christ, Son, Lord, only begotten, to be acknowledged in two natures, inconfusedly, unchangeably, indivisibly, inseparably;

the distinction of natures being by no means taken away by the union, but rather the property of each nature being preserved, and concurring in one Person and one Subsistence, not parted or divided into two persons, but one and the same Son, and only begotten God (*monogene theon*), the Word, the Lord Jesus Christ;

as the prophets from the beginning [have declared] concerning Him, and the Lord Jesus Christ Himself has taught us, and the Creed of the holy Fathers has handed down to us.

E. The Athanasian Creed

This creed was named after the important pastor and writer of the fourth century, Athanasius (293-373), but it was probably written in the fifth or sixth century, long after the time of Athanasius. In this text the term 'catholic' refers to all those Christians who did not follow one of the important heresies of the ancient world; the Christian church was not yet divided between Protestant and Roman Catholic, nor between eastern and western churches. It has been used by many Evangelical churches, though its didactic character makes it more suitable to a classroom or personal use than to a worship service.

Whosoever will be saved, before all things it is necessary that he hold the catholic faith. Which faith except every one do keep whole and undefiled; without doubt he shall perish everlastingly. And the catholic faith is this: That we worship one God in Trinity, and Trinity in Unity; Neither confounding the Persons; nor dividing the Essence. For there is one Person of the Father; another of the Son; and another of the Holy Ghost. But the Godhead of the Father, of the Son, and of the Holy Ghost, is all one; the Glory equal, the Majesty coeternal. Such as the Father is; such is the Son; and such is the Holy Ghost. The Father uncreated; the Son uncreated; and the Holy Ghost uncreated. The Father unlimited; the Son unlimited; and the Holy Ghost unlimited. The Father eternal; the Son eternal; and the Holy Ghost eternal. And yet they are not three eternals; but one eternal. As also there are not three uncreated; nor three infinites, but one uncreated; and one infinite. So likewise the Father is Almighty; the Son Almighty; and the Holy Ghost Almighty. And yet they are not three Almighties; but one Almighty. So the Father is God; the Son is God; and the Holy Ghost is God. And yet they are not three Gods; but one God. So likewise the Father is Lord; the Son Lord; and the Holy Ghost Lord. And yet not three Lords; but one Lord. For like as we are compelled by the Christian verity; to acknowledge every Person by himself to be God and Lord; So are we forbidden by the catholic religion; to say, There are three Gods, or three Lords. The Father is made of none; neither created, nor begotten. The Son is of the Father alone; not made, nor created; but begotten. The Holy Ghost is of the Father and of the Son; neither made, nor created, nor begotten; but proceeding. So there is one Father, not three Fathers; one Son, not three Sons; one Holy Ghost, not three Holy Ghosts. And in this Trinity none is before, or after another; none is greater, or less than another. But the whole three Persons are coeternal, and coequal. So that in all things, as aforesaid; the Unity in Trinity, and the Trinity in Unity, is to be worshipped. He therefore that will be saved, let him thus think of the Trinity.

Furthermore it is necessary to everlasting salvation; that he also believe faithfully the Incarnation of our Lord Jesus Christ. For the right Faith is, that we believe and confess; that our Lord Jesus Christ, the Son of God, is God and Man; God, of the Essence of the Father; begotten before the worlds; and Man, of the Essence of his Mother, born in the world. Perfect God; and perfect Man, of a reasonable soul and human flesh subsisting. Equal to the Father, as touching his Godhead; and inferior to the Father as touching his Manhood. Who although he is God and Man; yet he is not two, but one Christ. One; not by conversion of the Godhead into flesh; but by assumption of the Manhood by God. One altogether; not by confusion of Essence; but by unity of Person. For as the reasonable soul and flesh is one man; so God and Man is one Christ; Who suffered for our salvation; descended into hell; rose again the third day from the dead. He ascended into heaven, he sitteth on the right hand of the God the Father Almighty, from whence he will come to judge the quick and the dead. At whose coming all men will rise again with their bodies; And shall give account for their own works. And they that have done good shall go into life everlasting; and they that have done evil, into everlasting fire. This is the catholic faith; which except a man believe truly and firmly, he cannot be saved.

III The Trinity in the Medieval Reform Movements

While the various medieval reform movements within Christianity often focused on moral reforms and concerns regarding the sacraments, some of the many movements desired to be clear that their reforms were based on classical Christian doctrine. As an example we mention the Waldenses Confession of 1120. It not only explicitly affirms the Apostles' Creed; the fourteen articles of the Waldenses appear to be a development of the twelve articles of the *Apostolicum*.

1. We believe and firmly maintain all that is contained in the twelve articles of the symbol, commonly called the apostles' creed, and we regard as heretical whatever is inconsistent with the said twelve articles.

2. We believe that there is one God—the Father, Son, and Holy Spirit.

Appendix: The Trinity in the Bible and Selected Creeds of the Church

3. We acknowledge for sacred canonical scriptures the books of the Holy Bible. (Here follows the title of each, exactly conformable to our received canon, but which it is deemed, on that account, quite unnecessary to particularize.)

4. The books above-mentioned teach us: That there is one GOD, almighty, unbounded in wisdom, and infinite in goodness, and who, in His goodness, has made all things. For He created Adam after His own image and likeness. But through the enmity of the Devil, and his own disobedience, Adam fell, sin entered into the world, and we became transgressors in and by Adam.

5. That Christ had been promised to the fathers who received the law, to the end that, knowing their sin by the law, and their unrighteousness and insufficiency, they might desire the coming of Christ to make satisfaction for their sins, and to accomplish the law by Himself.

6. That at the time appointed of the Father, Christ was born—a time when iniquity everywhere abounded, to make it manifest that it was not for the sake of any good in ourselves, for all were sinners, but that He, who is true, might display His grace and mercy towards us.

7. That Christ is our life, and truth, and peace, and righteousness—our shepherd and advocate, our sacrifice and priest, who died for the salvation of all who should believe, and rose again for their justification.

8. And we also firmly believe, that there is no other mediator, or advocate with God the Father, but Jesus Christ. And as to the Virgin Mary, she was holy, humble, and full of grace; and this we also believe concerning all other saints, namely, that they are waiting in heaven for the resurrection of their bodies at the day of judgment.

9. We also believe, that, after this life, there are but two places—one for those that are saved, the other for the damned, which [two] we call paradise and hell, wholly denying that imaginary purgatory of Antichrist, invented in opposition to the truth.

10. Moreover, we have ever regarded all the inventions of men [in the affairs of religion] as an unspeakable abomination before God; such as the festival days and vigils of saints, and what is called holy-water, the abstaining from flesh on certain days, and such like things, but above all, the masses.

11. We hold in abhorrence all human inventions, as proceeding from Antichrist, which produce distress (Alluding probably to the voluntary penances and mortification imposed by the Catholics on themselves), and are prejudicial to the liberty of the mind.

12 We consider the Sacraments as signs of holy things, or as the visible emblems of invisible blessings. We regard it as proper and even necessary that believers use these symbols or visible forms when it can be done. Notwithstanding which, we maintain that believers may be saved without these signs, when they have neither place nor opportunity of observing them.

13. We acknowledge no sacraments [as of divine appointment] but baptism and the Lord's supper.

14. We honour the secular powers, with subjection, obedience, promptitude, and payment.[7]

IV The Trinity in Classical Protestant Confessions

From the beginnings of Protestantism, the ancient and classical doctrine of the Trinity was affirmed and taught as a central theme of the Christian faith. This is seen in the several branches of Protestantism that developed from the time of the Reformation in the 16th century. There is overwhelming consensus regarding the Trinity in the Protestant confessions. The following selections show that similarity among churches that had disagreements on questions regarding sacraments, liturgy, and other church policies.

A. The Augsburg Confession

This was and is the primary doctrinal standard of the Lutheran churches, written and officially accepted in 1530.

1] Our Churches, with common consent, do teach that the decree of the Council of Nicaea concerning the Unity of the Divine Essence and concerning the Three Persons, is true and to be believed without any doubting; 2] that is to say, there is one Divine Essence which is called and which is God: eternal, without body, without parts, of infinite power, wisdom, and goodness, the Maker and Preserver of all things, visible and invisible; and 3] yet there are three Persons, of the same essence and power, who also are coeternal, the Father, the Son, and the Holy Ghost. And the term 'person' 4] they use as the Fathers have used it, to signify, not a part or quality in another, but that which subsists of itself. 5] They condemn all heresies which have sprung up against this article, as the Manichaeans, who assumed two principles, one Good and the other Evil: also the Valentinians, Arians, Eunomians, Mohammedans, and all such. 6] They condemn also the Samosatenes, old and new, who, contending that there is but one Person, sophistically and impiously argue that the Word and the Holy Ghost are not distinct Persons, but that 'Word' signifies a spoken word, and 'Spirit' signifies motion created in things.

B. The Thirty Nine Articles of the Anglican Church

In 1562 the developing Church of England adopted its 'Thirty Nine Articles' which became its standard teaching. Its first two articles summarized the themes covered in the early statements of the church.

Article I: Of Faith in the Holy Trinity

There is but one living and true God, everlasting, without body, parts, or passions; of infinite power, wisdom, and goodness; the Maker, and Preserver of all

---

[7] http://www.freechurch.org/resources/confessions/waldenses.htm. Viewed 8 November, 2013.

things both visible and invisible. And in unity of this Godhead there be three Persons, of one substance, power, and eternity; the Father, the Son, and the Holy Ghost.

Article II: Of the Word or Son of God, which was made very Man

The Son, which is the Word of the Father, begotten from everlasting of the Father, the very and eternal God, and of one substance with the Father, took Man's nature in the womb of the blessed Virgin, of her substance: so that two whole and perfect Natures, that is to say, the Godhead and Manhood, were joined together in one Person, never to be divided, whereof is one Christ, very God, and very Man; who truly suffered, was crucified, dead, and buried, to reconcile His Father to us, and to be a sacrifice, not only for original guilt, but also for all actual sins of men.

C. The Second Helvetic Confession

This confession was written by Heinrich Bullinger in Switzerland in 1564 and enjoyed widespread use in Protestant churches in Scotland, Hungary, Poland, and France, as well as Switzerland. It shows the extent to which the Protestant Reformers were conscious of carefully following the early Christian creeds

GOD IS ONE. We believe and teach that God is one in essence or nature, subsisting in himself, all sufficient in himself, invisible, incorporeal, immense, eternal, Creator of all things both visible and invisible, the greatest good, living, quickening and preserving all things, omnipotent and supremely wise, kind and merciful, just and true. Truly we detest many gods because it is expressly written: 'The Lord your God is one Lord' (Deut.6:4). 'I am the Lord your God. You shall have no other gods before me' (Ex. 20:2-3). 'I am the Lord, and there is no other god besides me. Am I not the Lord, and there is no other God beside me? A righteous God and a Savior; there is none besides me' ((Isa. 45:5, 21). 'The Lord, the Lord, a God merciful and gracious, slow to anger, and abounding in steadfast love and faithfulness' (Ex. 34:6).

GOD IS THREE. Notwithstanding we believe and teach that the same immense, one and indivisible God is in person inseparably and without confusion distinguished as Father, Son and Holy Spirit so, as the Father has begotten the Son from eternity, the Son is begotten by an ineffable generation, and the holy Spirit truly proceeds from them both, and the same from eternity and is to be worshipped with both.

Thus there are not three gods, but three persons, cosubstantial, coeternal, and coequal; distinct with respect to hypostases, and with respect to order, the one preceding the other yet without any inequality. For according to the nature or essence they are so joined together that they are one God, and the divine nature is common to the Father, Son and Holy Spirit.

For Scripture has delivered to us a manifest distinction of persons, the angel saying, among other things, to the Blessed Virgin, 'The Holy Spirit will come upon you, and the power of the Most High will overshadow you; therefore the child to be born will be called holy, the Son of God' (Luke 1:35). And also in the baptism of Christ a voice is heard from heaven concerning Christ, saying, 'This is my beloved Son' (Math. 3:17). The Holy Spirit also appeared in the form of a dove (John 1:32). And when the Lord himself commanded the apostles to baptize, he commanded them to baptize 'in the name of the Father, and the Son, and the Holy Spirit' (Matt. 28:19). Elsewhere in the Gospel he said: 'The Father will send the Holy Spirit in my name' (John 14:26), and again he said: 'When the Counselor comes, whom I shall send to you from the Father, even the Spirit of truth, who proceeds from the Father, he will bear witness to me,' etc. (John 15:26). In short, we receive the Apostles' Creed because it delivers to us the true faith.

HERESIES. Therefore we condemn the Jews and Mohammedans, and all those who blaspheme that sacred and adorable Trinity. We also condemn all heresies and heretics who teach that the Son and Holy Spirit are God in name only, and also that there is something created and subservient, or subordinate to another in the Trinity, and that there is something unequal in it, a greater or a less, something corporeal or corporeally conceived, something different with respect to character or will, something mixed or solitary, as if the Son and Holy Spirit were the affections and properties of one God the Father, as the Monarchians, Novatians, Praxeas, Patripassians, Sabellius, Paul of Samosata, Aetius, Macedonius, Anthropomorphites, Arius, and such like, have thought.

D. The Bohemenian Confession of 1575

This confession has a slightly different character from some Reformation era documents because it was accepted by a very wide range of churches and Christians including the Hussite Ultraquists, the Unitas Fratrum (Unity of the Brethren) which was a Protestant Church from eastern Bohemia dating from 1457, along with some Lutherans and Roman Catholics. This confession articulates significant applications of the doctrine of the Trinity to the questions of the era: the second article of the Creed is applied to justification by faith in a manner one would expect from Lutherans and Calvinists while the third article of the Creed is applied to personal holiness and sanctification in a manner that looks forward to the Moravia Brethren, successors of the Unitas Fratrum, who later influenced John Wesley. This confession also includes both the preached Word and the Sacraments as applications of the basic confession about the Holy Spirit in the manner which was distinctive of the Reformation.

Of the Holy Trinity, or the Differences of Person in Divinity

1. We believe and confess, that the eternal God the Father is the first person of the Deity, omnipotent and eternal, of unfathomable and inconceivable power, wisdom, justice, holiness, and goodness, who from eternity begat a Son, the substantial and perfect image of his being, and from whom as well as from the Son comes the Holy Spirit, and who together with the Son and the Holy

Spirit was pleased to create all things visible and invisible from nothing in the acceptable time of his divine majesty, and according to his divine purpose provides, preserves, directs, and governs. And so concerning the divine being and substance as well as concerning the divine external acts, such as the creation, preservation, and direction of all things, we make no difference between the Father and the Son and the Holy Spirit.

2. We believe and with the mouth confess that the second person in the Deity, that is the eternal Son of God, our Lord Jesus Christ, was pleased to take on himself human nature in the body of the blessed Virgin Mary by the action of the Holy Spirit, so that dual nature divine and human in unity of person to eternal indivisibility is united, one Christ, true God and true man, born of the Virgin Mary, who for all human kind, truly suffered, was crucified, died, and was buried in order that he might reconcile us with God the Father. And he was the redeeming sacrifice not only for original sin, but also for all other sins that people commit. And this same Lord of ours, the divine Christ, descended into hell, and truly on the third day he rose from the dead for our justification. Afterward he ascended into heaven, sits on the right hand of God the Father, reigning eternally and ruling over all creation. He justifies all who believe in him, he sanctifies them, sending into their heart the Holy Spirit, who would rule, comfort, and revive them against the devil and the power of sin. And so he is the perfect mediator, advocate, and intercessor with God the Father, reconciler, redeemer, and Savior of his Church, which he gathers by the Holy Spirit, preserves, protects, and rules until completion of the number of the elect of God. Afterward that same Lord Christ will truly come again to judge the living and the dead in such manner as Christian faith and the Apostolic teaching declare more widely.

3. We believe and confess that the Holy Spirit is the third person in the Deity, from eternity coming from the Father and the Son, substantial and eternal, revealed as the Father's love to the Son, and as the Son's to the Father, as power and goodness inconceivable. He is seen not only in the creation and the preservation of all things, but also especially in those works which he pleased to do from the beginning of the Church in the sons of God, working in them through the ministry of the word of God, through the sacraments and the living faith to eternal salvation which is deposited in God's elect in Lord Christ from the foundation of the world.[8]

E. The London Baptist Confession of 1689

Because this confession is a century later than the first Reformation confessions but carefully repeats the same themes of the earlier Protestant confessions, it shows the tremendous extent to which the several branches of Protestantism

---

[8] http://moravianarchives.org/wp-content/uploads/2012/01/Bohemian-Confession-1575.pdf. Viewed 8 November, 2013.

shared a highly developed doctrine of the Trinity which was regarded as foundational to the Christian faith.

God and the Holy Trinity

The Lord our God is the one and only living and true God; Whose subsistence is in and of Himself

- Who is infinite in being and perfection; Whose essence cannot be comprehended by any but Himself;

- Who is a most pure spirit, invisible, without body, parts, or passions

- Who only has immortality

- Who dwells in the light which no man can approach, Who is immutable, immense, eternal, incomprehensible, almighty, in every way infinite, most holy, most wise, most free, most absolute;

- Who works all things according to the counsel of His own immutable and most righteous will, for His own glory;

- Who is most loving, gracious, merciful, longsuffering, and abundant in goodness and truth;

- Who forgives iniquity, transgression, and sin;

- Who is the rewarder of those who diligently seek Him;

- and Who, at the same time, is most just and terrible in His judgements, hating all sin and Who will by no means clear the guilty.

God, having all life, glory, goodness, blessedness, in and from Himself, is unique in being all- sufficient, both in Himself and to Himself, not standing in need of any creature which He has made, nor deriving any glory from such.

- On the contrary, it is God Who manifests His own glory in them, through them, to them and upon them. He is the only fountain of all being; from Whom, through Whom, and to Whom all things exist and move.

- He has completely sovereign dominion over all creatures, to do through them, for them, or to them whatever He pleases.

- In His sight all things are open and manifest; His knowledge is infinite, infallible, and not dependent on the creature.

- Therefore, nothing is for Him contingent or uncertain.

- He is most holy in all His counsels, in all His works, and in all His commands.

- To Him is due from angels and men whatever worship, service, or obedience, they owe as creatures to the Creator, and whatever else He is pleased to require from them.

In this divine and infinite Being there are three subsistences, the Father, the Word or Son, and the Holy Spirit. All are one in substance, power, and eternity; each having the whole divine essence, yet this essence being undivided.

The Father was not derived from any other being; He was neither brought into being by, nor did He issue from any other being.

- The Son is eternally begotten of the Father.
- The Holy Spirit proceeds from the Father and the Son.
- All three are infinite, without beginning, and are therefore only one God, Who is not to be divided in nature and being, but distinguished by several peculiar relative properties, and also their personal relations.
- This doctrine of the Trinity is the foundation of all our communion with God, and our comfortable dependence on Him.

V The Doctrine of the Trinity, Recent Developments

A striking characteristic of the global evangelical missions movement of the 20th and 21st centuries has been the serious thinking about the doctrine of the Trinity which both builds on the classical statements and then understands the calling of Christians and of the church in light of Trinitarian doctrine. We include two examples, from Amsterdam 2000 and Capetown 2012.

A. The Amsterdam Declaration 2000

1. God

The God of whom this Declaration speaks is the self-revealed Creator, Upholder, Governor and Lord of the universe. This God is eternal in his self-existence and unchanging in his holy love, goodness, justice, wisdom, and faithfulness to his promises. God in his own being is a community of three coequal and coeternal persons, who are revealed to us in the Bible as the Father, the Son, and the Holy Spirit. Together they are involved in an unvarying cooperative pattern in all God's relationships to and within this world. God is Lord of history, where he blesses his own people, overcomes and judges human and angelic rebels against his rule, and will finally renew the whole created order.

2. Jesus Christ

The Declaration takes the view of Jesus that the canonical New Testament sets forth and the historic Christian creeds and confessions attest. He was, and is, the second person of the triune Godhead, now and forever incarnate. He was virgin-born, lived a life of perfect godliness, died on the cross as the substitutionary sacrifice for our sins, was raised bodily from the dead, ascended into heaven, reigns now over the universe and will personally return for judgment and the renewal of all things. As the God-man, once crucified, now enthroned, he is the Lord and Savior who in love fulfills towards us the threefold mediational ministry of prophet, priest and king. His title, 'Christ,' proclaims him the anointed servant of God who fulfills all the Messianic hopes of the canonical Old Testament.

3. Holy Spirit

Shown by the words of Jesus to be the third divine person, whose name, 'Spirit,' pictures the energy of breath and wind, the Holy Spirit is the dynamic personal presence of the Trinity in the processes of the created world, in the communication of divine truth, in the attesting of Jesus Christ, in the new creation through him of believers and of the church, and in ongoing fellowship and service. The fullness of the ministry of the Holy Spirit in relation to the knowledge of Christ and the enjoyment of new life in him dates from the Pentecostal outpouring recorded in Acts 2. As the divine inspirer and interpreter of the Bible, the Spirit empowers God's people to set forth accurate, searching, life-transforming presentations of the gospel of Jesus Christ, and makes their communication a fruitful means of grace to their hearers. The New Testament shows us the supernatural power of the Spirit working miracles, signs and wonders, bestowing gifts of many kinds, and overcoming the power of Satan in human lives for the advancement of the gospel. Christians agree that the power of the Holy Spirit is vitally necessary for evangelism and that openness to his ministry should mark all believers.[9]

B. The Capetown Commitment of 2010

This newest main document of the global missions movement, released at the Third Lausanne Congress on World Evangelisation in October 2010, also displays a developed doctrine of the Trinity which builds on the statements of the early church. Not surprisingly, the practical application of the Trinitarian understanding of God is primarily related to world missions.

Article 3. We love God the Father

Through Jesus Christ, God's Son,—and through him alone as the way, the truth and the life—we come to know and love God as Father. As the Holy Spirit testifies with our spirit that we are God's children, so we cry the words Jesus prayed, 'Abba, Father', and we pray the prayer Jesus taught, 'Our Father'. Our love for Jesus, proved by obeying him, is met by the Father's love for us as the Father and the Son make their home in us, in mutual giving and receiving of love. This intimate relationship has deep biblical foundations.

Article 4. We love God the Son

God commanded Israel to love the LORD God with exclusive loyalty. Likewise for us, loving the Lord Jesus Christ means that we steadfastly affirm that he alone is Saviour, Lord and God. The Bible teaches that Jesus performs the same sovereign actions as God alone. Christ is Creator of the universe, Ruler of history, Judge of all nations and Saviour of all who turn to God. He shares the identity of God in the divine equality and unity of Father, Son and Holy Spirit. Just as God called Israel to love him in covenantal faith, obedience and servant-witness, we affirm our love for Jesus Christ by trusting in him, obeying him, and making him known.

---

9 http://www.christianitytoday.com/ct/2000/augustweb-only/13.0.html?start=6. Viewed 9 November, 2013.

Article 5. We love God the Holy Spirit

We love the Holy Spirit within the unity of the Trinity, along with God the Father and God the Son. He is the missionary Spirit sent by the missionary Father and the missionary Son, breathing life and power into God's missionary Church. We love and pray for the presence of the Holy Spirit because without the witness of the Spirit to Christ, our own witness is futile. Without the convicting work of the Spirit, our preaching is in vain. Without the gifts, guidance and power of the Spirit, our mission is mere human effort. And without the fruit of the Spirit, our unattractive lives cannot reflect the beauty of the gospel.

C. Recent Mennonite Theology and Ethics

Though some early Mennonite confessions, such as the Schleitheim Confession of 1527, did not discuss the Trinity at length, this gap has been very competently addressed in recent times. As an example we include the version of the Confession of Faith of the Canadian Mennonite Brethren Church (2004).

We believe in the one, true, living God, Creator of heaven and earth. God is almighty in power, perfect in wisdom, righteous in judgment, overflowing in steadfast love. God is the Sovereign who rules over all things visible and invisible, the Shepherd who rescues the lost and helpless. God is a refuge and fortress for those in need. God is a consuming fire, perfect in holiness, yet slow to anger and abounding in tender mercy. God comforts like a loving mother, trains and disciplines like a caring father, and persists in covenant love like a faithful husband. We confess God as eternal Father, Son, and Holy Spirit.

God the Father

God the Father is the source of all life. In Him we live and move and have our being. The Father seeks those who will worship Him in spirit and in truth, and hears the prayers of all who call on Him. In the fullness of time, the Father sent the Son for the salvation of the world. Through Jesus Christ the Father adopts all who respond in faith to the gospel, forgiving those who repent of their sin and entering into a new covenant with them. God gives the Counselor, the Holy Spirit, to all His children. God's creative and redemptive love sustains this world until the end of the age.

God the Son

The Son, through whom all things were created and who holds all things together, is the image of the invisible God. Conceived by the Holy Spirit and born of the virgin Mary, Jesus took on human nature to redeem this fallen world. He revealed the fullness of God through his obedient and sinless life. Through word and deed Jesus proclaimed the reign of God, bringing good news to the poor, release to the captives, and recovery of sight to the blind. Christ triumphed over sin through His death and resurrection, and was exalted as Lord of creation and the church. The Savior of the world invites all to be reconciled to God, offering peace to those far and near, and calling them to follow Him in the way of the cross. Until the Lord Jesus returns in glory, He intercedes for believers, acts as their advocate, and calls them to be His witnesses.

God the Holy Spirit

The Holy Spirit, the Counselor, is the creative power, presence and wisdom of God. The Spirit convicts people of sin, gives them new life, and guides them into all truth. By the Spirit believers are baptized into one body. The indwelling Spirit testifies that they are God's children, distributes gifts for ministry, empowers for witness, and produces the fruit of righteousness. As Comforter, the Holy Spirit helps God's children in their weakness, intercedes for them according to God's will and assures them of eternal life. [10]

D. The Filioque: A Church Dividing Issue? An Agreed Statement, 2003

One of the continuing discussions between the Orthodox and Roman Catholic churches has been whether or not the filioque clause should be included in the Nicene-Constantinopolitan Creed of 381. Evangelicals and Protestants have generally followed the western or Roman Catholic version of this creed, though not with 100% consistency. Evangelical teachers should take note of this selection from the North American Orthodox-Catholic Consultation, 2003.

We are aware that the problem of the theology of the Filioque, and its use in the Creed, is not simply an issue between the Catholic and Orthodox communions. Many Protestant Churches, too, drawing on the theological legacy of the Medieval West, consider the term to represent an integral part of the orthodox Christian confession. Although dialogue among a number of these Churches and the Orthodox communion has already touched on the issue, any future resolution of the disagreement between East and West on the origin of the Spirit must involve all those communities that profess the Creed of 381 as a standard of faith. Aware of its limitations, our Consultation nonetheless makes the following theological and practical recommendations to the members and the bishops of our own Churches:

- that our Churches commit themselves to a new and earnest dialogue concerning the origin and person of the Holy Spirit, drawing on the Holy Scriptures and on the full riches of the theological traditions of both our Churches, and to looking for constructive ways of expressing what is central to our faith on this difficult issue;
- that all involved in such dialogue expressly recognize the limitations of our ability to make definitive assertions about the inner life of God;
- that in the future, because of the progress in mutual understanding that has come about in recent decades, Orthodox and Catholics refrain from labeling

---

10 http://www.mbconf.ca/resource/File/PDFs/Confession_of_Faith_v.1.pdf. Viewed 8 November, 2013.

as heretical the traditions of the other side on the subject of the procession of the Holy Spirit;
- that Orthodox and Catholic theologians distinguish more clearly between the divinity and hypostatic identity of the Holy Spirit, which is a received dogma of our Churches, and the manner of the Spirit's origin, which still awaits full and final ecumenical resolution;
- that those engaged in dialogue on this issue distinguish, as far as possible, the theological issues of the origin of the Holy Spirit from the ecclesiological issues of primacy and doctrinal authority in the Church, even as we pursue both questions seriously together;
- that the theological dialogue between our Churches also give careful consideration to the status of later councils held in both our Churches after those seven generally received as ecumenical.
- that the Catholic Church, as a consequence of the normative and irrevocable dogmatic value of the Creed of 381, use the original Greek text alone in making translations of that Creed for catechetical and liturgical use.
- that the Catholic Church, following a growing theological consensus, and in particular the statements made by Pope Paul VI, declare that the condemnation made at the Second Council of Lyons (1274) of those 'who presume to deny that the Holy Spirit proceeds eternally from the Father and the Son' is no longer applicable.

We offer these recommendations to our Churches in the conviction, based on our own intense study and discussion, that our traditions' different ways of understanding the procession of the Holy Spirit need no longer divide us. We believe, rather, that our profession of the ancient Creed of Constantinople must be allowed to become, by our uniform practice and our new attempts at mutual understanding, the basis for a more conscious unity in the one faith that all theology simply seeks to clarify and to deepen. Although our expression of the truth God reveals about his own Being must always remain limited by the boundaries of human understanding and human words, we believe that it is the very 'Spirit of truth,' whom Jesus breathes upon his Church, who remains with us still, to 'guide us into all truth' (John 16.13). We pray that our Churches' understanding of this Spirit may no longer be a scandal to us, or an obstacle to unity in Christ, but that the one truth towards which he guides us may truly be 'a bond of peace' (Eph 4.3), for us and for all Christians.[11]

---

11 http://www.usccb.org/beliefs-and-teachings/ecumenical-and-interreligious/ecumenical/orthodox/filioque-church-dividing-issue-english.cfm. Viewed 14 November 2013.

World Evangelical Alliance

World Evangelical Alliance is a global ministry working with local churches around the world to join in common concern to live and proclaim the Good News of Jesus in their communities. WEA is a network of churches in 129 nations that have each formed an evangelical alliance and over 100 international organizations joining together to give a worldwide identity, voice and platform to more than 600 million evangelical Christians. Seeking holiness, justice and renewal at every level of society – individual, family, community and culture, God is glorified and the nations of the earth are forever transformed.

Christians from ten countries met in London in 1846 for the purpose of launching, in their own words, "a new thing in church history, a definite organization for the expression of unity amongst Christian individuals belonging to different churches." This was the beginning of a vision that was fulfilled in 1951 when believers from 21 countries officially formed the World Evangelical Fellowship. Today, 150 years after the London gathering, WEA is a dynamic global structure for unity and action that embraces 600 million evangelicals in 129 countries. It is a unity based on the historic Christian faith expressed in the evangelical tradition. And it looks to the future with vision to accomplish God's purposes in discipling the nations for Jesus Christ.

Commissions:

- Theology
- Missions
- Religious Liberty
- Women's Concerns
- Youth
- Information Technology

Initiatives and Activities

- Ambassador for Human Rights
- Ambassador for Refugees
- Creation Care Task Force
- Global Generosity Network
- International Institute for Religious Freedom
- International Institute for Islamic Studies
- Leadership Institute
- Micah Challenge
- Global Human Trafficking Task Force
- Peace and Reconciliation Initiative
- UN-Team

Church Street Station
P.O. Box 3402
New York, NY 10008-3402
Phone +[1] 212 233 3046
Fax +[1] 646-957-9218
www.worldea.org

Giving Hands

GIVING HANDS GERMANY (GH) was established in 1995 and is officially recognized as a nonprofit foreign aid organization. It is an international operating charity that – up to now – has been supporting projects in about 40 countries on four continents. In particular we care for orphans and street children. Our major focus is on Africa and Central America. GIVING HANDS always mainly provides assistance for self-help and furthers human rights thinking.

The charity itself is not bound to any church, but on the spot we are cooperating with churches of all denominations. Naturally we also cooperate with other charities as well as governmental organizations to provide assistance as effective as possible under the given circumstances.

The work of GIVING HANDS GERMANY is controlled by a supervisory board. Members of this board are Manfred Feldmann, Colonel V. Doner and Kathleen McCall. Dr. Christine Schirrmacher is registered as legal manager of GIVING HANDS at the local district court. The local office and work of the charity are coordinated by Rev. Horst J. Kreie as executive manager. Dr. theol. Thomas Schirrmacher serves as a special consultant for all projects.

Thanks to our international contacts companies and organizations from many countries time and again provide containers with gifts in kind which we send to the different destinations where these goods help to satisfy elementary needs. This statutory purpose is put into practice by granting nutrition, clothing, education, construction and maintenance of training centers at home and abroad, construction of wells and operation of water treatment systems, guidance for self-help and transportation of goods and gifts to areas and countries where needy people live.

GIVING HANDS has a publishing arm under the leadership of Titus Vogt, that publishes human rights and other books in English, Spanish, Swahili and other languages.

These aims are aspired to the glory of the Lord according to the basic Christian principles put down in the Holy Bible.

Baumschulallee 3a • D-53115 Bonn • Germany
Phone: +49 / 228 / 695531 • Fax +49 / 228 / 695532
www.gebende-haende.de • info@gebende-haende.de

Martin Bucer Seminary

**Faithful to biblical truth
Cooperating with the Evangelical Alliance
Reformed**

Solid training for the Kingdom of God
- Alternative theological education
- Study while serving a church or working another job
- Enables students to remain in their own churches
- Encourages independent thinking
- Learning from the growth of the universal church.

Academic
- For the Bachelor's degree: 180 Bologna-Credits
- For the Master's degree: 120 additional Credits
- Both old and new teaching methods: All day seminars, independent study, term papers, etc.

Our Orientation:
- Complete trust in the reliability of the Bible
- Building on reformation theology
- Based on the confession of the German Evangelical Alliance
- Open for innovations in the Kingdom of God

Our Emphasis:
- The Bible
- Ethics and Basic Theology
- Missions
- The Church

Our Style:
- Innovative
- Relevant to society
- International
- Research oriented
- Interdisciplinary

Structure
- 15 study centers in 7 countries with local partners
- 5 research institutes
- President: Prof. Dr. Thomas Schirrmacher
  Vice President: Prof. Dr. Thomas K. Johnson
- Deans: Thomas Kinker, Th.D.;
  Titus Vogt, lic. theol., Carsten Friedrich, M.Th.

Missions through research
- Institute for Religious Freedom
- Institute for Islamic Studies
- Institute for Life and Family Studies
- Institute for Crisis, Dying, and Grief Counseling
- Institute for Pastoral Care

www.bucer.eu • info@bucer.eu

Berlin I Bielefeld I Bonn I Chemnitz I Hamburg I Munich I Pforzheim
Innsbruck I Istanbul I Izmir I Linz I Prague I São Paulo I Tirana I Zurich

www.ingramcontent.com/pod-product-compliance
Lightning Source LLC
Chambersburg PA
CBHW070323100426
42743CB00011B/2540